3F

REVENGE
OF
America's
UNEMPLOYED

RICHARD S. SLOAN

Revenge of America's Unemployed

Copyright © 2016 by Richard S. Sloan

Print ISBN: 978-1-48359-642-6

eBook ISBN: 978-1-48359-643-3

Cover Photograph: Bill Burke

First Printing 2017

Printed and Bound in the United States

ACKNOWLEDGEMENTS

To the more than 400,000 Facebook activists who "liked" the Union of Unemployed's page and "shared" its posts with friends and family members, I owe the deepest sense of gratitude. You helped break the isolation the unemployed so often feel as they search for work. But you did far more, you changed America's politics, perhaps forever.

In elections from 2008 to 2016, the unemployed, underemployed and uncounted came out to vote in unprecedented numbers. They voted their hopes, then their angst, then their frustrations and, finally, their fierce anger at being ignored. They survived the worst ravages of the Great Recession, but barely, only to find out that the party of FDR had moved on. And yet, the jobs activists on UCubed never did. They fought above their weight as a *New York Times* reporter remarked. In what became the trench warfare of social media, they never gave an inch. For that, I will be ever indebted to the hundreds and thousands who stuck with me.

Throughout the darkest days of the Great Recession, Tom Buffenbarger and Leo Hindery stood by my efforts to organize the unemployed into a potent political force. So did my son, Chris Sloan, whose political skills guided me along the way. Patrick Halley, who served as lead advance for Hillary Clinton for a decade, was the irreplaceable friend, colleague, advisor and editor throughout this amazing journey. The creative talents of Ian Lurie, Glenn Totten, LaToya Egwuekwe, Dan Grady and Ben Waxman, who served with Pat Halley on the UCubed Board of Directors, were on display every day for seven years. And the photography of Bill Burke, Suzannah Hoover and Cindy Truitt, the social media skills of Joyce Sheppard, Keith Breitbach, Tracy Beach and Alex DeLeon, the graphic artistry of Adele Polis, the Spanish language translations of Rugy Ogno and the research done by Stephen Seifert brought to life the thousands of posts, photos, memes and videos that drew millions to our Facebook pages.

And yet, were it not for the inspiration, friendship, wisdom and tenacity of six women this book could never have been written. Closest to my heart are Katie, Jenn and Mo whose own examples of drive and determination spurred me on through the toughest times. Kathleen and Lissa offered timely, sound and sage advice. And every day from page one until the final paragraph, Hillary provided the storyline of the endurance and tenacity needed to fight against incredible odds. She was — and remains — an inspiration for me and millions here and around the world.

That I failed her is my most important acknowledgement. That I could not persuade her campaign to focus on those jobless households and working class Democrats whose votes she lost is all on me. And I fear that their revenge, as the poet John Milton reminds us, "at first though sweet, bitter ere long back on itself recoils."

To Katie

TABLE OF CONTENTS

ABOUT THE AUTHOR

Rick Sloan is a thoughtful, provocative strategist with a rare genius for drawing large insights from the smallest details of America's electoral past. At the height of the Great Recession, he created and then led the Union of Unemployed (nicknamed UCubed) until his retirement.

Launched in early 2010, his virtual union grew to 450,000 Facebook activists by 2015, engaged 15 million users and reached 213 million fans and their friends that year. Its Facebook-centric campaigns in 2010, 2012, and 2014 used animated cartoons to skewer Republicans and their Tea Party allies. In early 2016, its memes, posts and videos offered a useful perspective on politics for the jobless … and a unique Get Out The Vote strategy for a presidential campaign.

Sloan's career spans four decades and eleven presidential campaigns, two stints on Capitol Hill as Chief of Staff to the late Senator Howard Metzenbaum from Ohio and then Michigan Congressman John Dingell, his own campaign against then Ohio Congressman John Kasich in 1984, and nearly 30 years working for (and with) progressive labor unions. He is the author of *The Gift of Strategy*. Published in 1995, the book urged Democrats to focus on a Steel and Seaboard Strategy, deepening the party's ties to the industrial Midwest and the coasts, and to the old and new Democrats who lived there. And with *Revenge of America's Unemployed*, he brings his career to a close.

Rick Sloan was born in Erie, Pennsylvania. He received his B.A. and J.D degrees from The Ohio State University. He now lives in Washington, D.C. with his wife, Katrinka Smith Sloan. Their three adult children, Christopher, Jennifer and Moria, are pursuing careers in pubic policy and public health.

PROLOGUE

BE THEIR CHAMPION

In late March 2015, three weeks before Hillary Clinton announced her 2016 presidential campaign, I posted an open letter to her on the UCubed Facebook page and website. UCubed was the nickname for the Union of Unemployed, a virtual union launched in mid-January 2010 as a community service project of the International Association of Machinists and Aerospace Workers. The letter reprised a memo I had written in 2010 to friends who were nationally recognized advocates for women's rights. The memo raised an issue that was getting scant coverage at the time—the rising level of domestic violence tied to joblessness.

I began the letter to Secretary Clinton saying, "Your sisters are hurting. So are their children. And yet, no one seems to care how insidiously cruel the Great Recession became for millions of Americans." My letter ended with the plea, "In the darkness enveloping them, they pray for a champion. Please, please, be their champion."

To my surprise, at the end of Hillary Clinton's pre-announcement video, which began with a collage of American families getting ready to take on new challenges, she looked directly into the camera and said, "Every day Americans need a champion. And I want to be that champion." She used the phrase again in her formal announcement speech on Roosevelt Island in New York the following day. Surrounded by thousands of supporters crowding into a park dedicated to FDR's Four Freedoms, Hillary's speech focused on the economy and jobs and appealed to the broad middle class.

Secretary Clinton was the first Democrat to enter the race. Vermont Senator Bernie Sanders and former Maryland Governor Martin O'Malley would announce their candidacies in late May. Fourteen Republicans had already been announced when Hillary for America released that pre-announcement video. Donald Trump entered the race four days after she did. And in July, Ohio Governor John Kasich and former Virginia Governor Jim Gilmore would make the GOP field of seventeen candidates, the largest ever.

Her campaign's phrasing was awkward—would she be a champion for everyday Americans? Or would she be America's champion every day? This meant that the theme lasted only a few months. It became just one of the dozens that Hillary for America trotted out and then discarded in its search for a message that resonated with the American people.

Divorced from the harsh realities that led to my plea for a champion, the ensuing turmoil over themes lost all meaning. For mere words held no magic power. Only the people who needed a champion did. Having been scarred so deeply by the Great Recession, they held the power to make or break Hillary Clinton's presidential campaign.

Describing how the lives of America's unemployed, underemployed and uncounted intersected with Hillary Clinton's two campaigns for the White House is the primary purpose of this book. To a lesser degree, it recounts my own efforts to create a virtual union. And it represents another, longer plea to future presidential candidates to think deeply about why so many working class Democrats have shifted their allegiances over the last decade.

So, before launching into the beginning of this story, it would be useful to provide readers with that original open letter from March 30, 2015.

Dear Secretary Clinton:

Your sisters are hurting. So are their children. And yet, no one seems to care how insidiously cruel the Great Recession became for millions of Americans.

Five years ago, the media shifted away from the jobless to cover other stories competing for national attention. The unemployed and underemployed became old news. So their heartbreaking stories seldom saw the light of day.

Yet, invisibility did not make their pain go away. That invisibility only escalated its economic, emotional and physical toll. In this news blackout, an evil darkness descended on home after home.

In each family with a jobless adult, the pressure on the adult female grew intense. If she was working and her spouse was not, the family dynamic[s] changed. Tensions rose as money grew tight and exploded over little things when the shelves grew bare. As months turned into years, self-worth turned to self-loathing for herself and disgust at her spouse.

If her spouse was working and she was not working, the difference between a pay stub and an unemployment check put the family on a down escalator from the middle to the working class or, all too often, the working poor. Only one-third of the jobless women qualified for unemployment insurance. As a result, the bills went unpaid, the credit cards maxed out, and each unexpected expense became a flashpoint.

Losing the emotional security that comes from working, from having a job to go to, caused much of the unseen pain within the immediate family circle. But it did not stop there. As their downward trajectory accelerated, the children, grandparents, godparents, in-laws and even neighbors were drawn into the vortex.

At the height of the Great Recession, 15 million Americans were unemployed and another 15 or 16 million were underemployed or had left the workforce entirely. Those massive numbers, however, masked how broadly and deeply the pain was shared. It hit home after home, neighborhood after neighborhood.

While reports of suicides and domestic violence mounted, the far more pervasive trauma came in the psychological pounding these women and children took. Five years ago, Rutgers' Center for Workforce Development released "No End in Sight: The Agony of Prolonged Unemployment." In their report, the researchers wrote:

> "The emotional upheaval felt by those who have been looking for work for so long range from physical distress to isolation and, worse, substance abuse ... [Almost] half say they avoid social contact with family, friends[,] and acquaintances, while 44% have now lost contact with close friends. Forty-three percent say they are quick to anger and 13% of the unemployed now report substance dependency.

> Respondents express in the strongest personal terms the personal toll being exacted when they are asked about the most difficult thing about being unemployed. Many of the comments evidence a lack of self-worth, shrinking self-esteem, a diminished sense of self-confidence, and isolation."

The Rutgers' study did not focus exclusively on women and their children. But its findings could mean only one thing: five years ago, they were living with the kind of emotional pain that only a return to work could erase. Now, five years later, millions still carry those emotional scars and still wait for the recovery to reach them.

And there's the rub.

We *cannot* ease their pain without replacing the 11.2 million jobs lost in the recession.

We *cannot* wait for the GDP to grow at more than 3.5 percent, for that will take far, far too long to produce 11.2 million jobs.

We *cannot* enact a major jobs initiative in this Congress given the "just say no" approach of Republican Senators and Representatives toward stimulus programs.

We *cannot* produce the Democratic majorities in the follow-on Congresses without those jobless households being convinced that our nominee and party have a plan to put millions to work.

We *cannot* persuade the jobless that we are on their side unless we seek them out, listen to their stories and probe for more information.

And, if we *cannot* empathize with the single moms and unemployed spouses struggling to feed and clothe their children, why should they even care what we have to say?

Secretary Clinton, this Gordian Knot of *cannots* can only be cut by a Democratic nominee willing to address the economic and emotional pain still darkening the homes of the unemployed.

In fact, it is the *only* way we can add sufficient numbers to our congressional caucuses to produce the all-of-government approach needed to create new jobs and new industries.

And frankly, you are the only one who can cut that knot.

So, at the first opportunity, lay out your plans to alleviate the economic and emotional pain millions of Americans have experienced since your last campaign.

Please, your sisters are hurting. Their kids suffer. In the darkness enveloping them, they pray for a champion.

Please, please, be their champion.

I signed the letter as CEO of the Union of Unemployed, an organization with 360,000 Facebook activists in March 2015 that did not exist when the Great Recession began to gather its mass and momentum in the summer of 2007.

CHAPTER 1

CRYING WOLF EVER SO SOFTLY

I did everything right, or thought I had. I saved money, I worked hard, I had a down payment, I got a house, I was working toward that "American Dream" and then it all disappeared.

Kristine's Unemployment Story

Global financial markets and central banks are not something most labor leaders had ever paid much attention to on a daily basis. But in August 2007, it was hard ignore the news reports of central bankers in London, Bonn, Tokyo and Washington injecting billions of dollars, euros and yen into their banking systems to avert a worldwide liquidity crisis.

As the communications director of Machinists, a union with roughly 400,000 dues-paying members in the United States and Canada, my day job entailed editing a magazine, overseeing a television studio, managing a massive website, preparing for its presidential endorsement and other duties as assigned. Under that last category, its international president, R. Thomas Buffenbarger, had me staffing him on meetings of the AFL-CIO Executive Council and Finance Committee.

So my interest in what the central bankers were doing had been piqued six months earlier when HSBC announced losses linked to subprime loans in the United States. One of the world's largest banking conglomerates, HSBC was of special interest to the American labor movement.

HSBC's affinity credit cards could be found in the wallets of nearly 2 million union members with balances in excess of $6.5 billion. Thousands of Machinists carried those HSBC cards.

Having sat in on the federation's Finance Committee for more than five years, I knew that those HSBC cards generated roughly $56 million every year, split evenly between the AFL-CIO and its 58 affiliated unions. Those royalty payments represented one-sixth of the AFL-CIO's annual revenues but a much smaller share of its affiliates' revenue streams. So, when HSBC announced that it took a huge loss on its subprime loans, my radar screens lit up.

Every other month or so, another odd but related story to subprime lending would grace the business pages. In April, New Century Financial filed for bankruptcy and cut half its workforce. In May, Ben Bernanke, the Federal Reserve Chairman, reported that mortgage defaults would not *seriously* harm the economy. In June, two hedge funds run by Bear Stearns and specializing in subprime mortgages faced large losses, dumped assets and sought help from other Wall Street firms that had lent money to those hedge funds. A month later, Bear Stearns told its investors that rival banks had refused to come to their rescue.

Then all hell broke loose in Europe. BNP Paribas, a global bank headquartered in Paris, shuttered two funds claiming a *complete evaporation of liquidity*. The European Central Bank pumped €203 billion—about $284 billion—into the market over two days. Within weeks, Germany's Sachensen Landesbank barely survived and IKB lost a billion dollars, both due to subprime loans originating in the United States.

Between September 1 and October 30, Northern Rock in Britain, UBS in Switzerland along with Citigroup and Merrill Lynch in the United States announced loses due to subprime loans approaching $20 billion. That figure tripled in the coming months.

Meanwhile, the Federal Reserve had cut its main interest rate from 6.25 to 4.75 percent. And Ben *Nothing-To-Worry-About* Bernake and his central banker colleagues kept pumping hundreds of billions into global markets trying to end the liquidity crisis, a crisis befuddling even the most astute central bankers.

Called to account before Parliament, the Bank of England's highest ranking official was forced to admit he had no idea what credit default swaps or credit default obligations were. Much to his chagrin, those credit default obligations or CDOs and credit default swaps or CDSs had grown exponentially over the past decade. Literally trillions of dollars of these almost worthless pieces of commercial paper were printed, broken into tranches with stolid, reassuring names and sold to the gurus of high finance around the world.

Never had so many brilliant men and women been so gullible. There was even a study done by three Rutgers University graduate students proving, mathematically and beyond any doubt, that there was zero risk in such an investment strategy. They had an entire page of equations to make their point. It was totally convincing and completely wrong.

And that's when the WARN notices started landing in working class homes. As required by a law written by the late US Senator Howard M. Meztenbaum, an Ohio Democrat, businesses with more than 100 full-time workers were required to give their workers a 60-day notice before closing a plant, laying off 50 full-time workers at a single site, or doing a mass lay-off of 50 to 499 workers. Those notices allowed workers to plan ahead and, in a vibrant economy, start their job search.

Between August 31 and December 31, 2007, nearly 7,200 American workers received WARN notices. In the first three months of 2008, just as the presidential primaries and caucuses began, another 5,700 men and women received their 60 days' notices. By election day 2008, another 11,300 WARN notices were issued.

Those WARN notices were but the tip of the proverbial iceberg. The WARN act had a catch. It did not apply to *unforeseen business circumstances*. And a global liquidity crisis, one that had central bankers working feverishly but futilely in August 2007, qualified as such an unforeseen event.

To the millions of small businesses not covered by the legislation and the thousands that employed more than 100 full-time workers, there were no legal requirements to provide any warning at all. Most of them were kept completely in the dark that summer by Ben Bernacke and his central banker buddies. Another year would go by before the US economy slammed into the iceberg and tens of millions of Americans were left trapped below decks.

Meanwhile, the 2008 presidential race continued apace. As the nation looked toward a Labor Day weekend filled with ballgames, car sales and family cookouts, four presidential candidates headed to Orlando, Florida, to vie for the Machinists' first dual presidential political endorsement. The twelve candidates invited to the union's conversations with the candidate were evenly split: half were Republicans and the other half were Democrats. Senators John Edwards (D-NC) and Hillary Clinton (D-NY), Congressman Dennis Kucinich (D-OH) and former Governor Mike Huckabee (R-AR) accepted the union's invitation. Notably, Senators Barack Obama and Joe Biden declined.

CHAPTER 2

CONVERSATIONS WITH THE CANDIDATES

I truly feel like I am reliving my grandparents' depression where they lived with family. I can't even afford blood pressure medicine or to get my fractured tooth fixed. I live on Advil and aspirin. It is depressing.

Jennifer's Unemployment Story

Candidates running for president hone their stump speeches in the living rooms and kitchens of supporters in Iowa and New Hampshire. Their answers to the neighbors' questions often come across as genuine, completely responsive and deeply thoughtful. And yet, like their stump speeches, those answers are little more than a rote recitation of their talking points. Practiced day after day on people who seldom see a state senator or county executive let alone a United States senator or governor, the answers come across as unique, off-the-cuff and spot-on.

Clearly the politicians who trek through the sweltering heat of Iowa or the snows of New Hampshire a year (or two) before their First-in-the-Nation caucus or primary have their lines down pat. Most can anticipate where the questioner is headed even before their question is asked. If a question touches on a sensitive subject, the politician might even interrupt the questioner and give an answer to a slightly different question or even an unasked question. By doing so, they stay on message and avoid political pitfalls.

Senator John Edwards of North Carolina, a former trial lawyer and the Democratic vice presidential nominee in 2004, was a pro at anticipating dangerous questions. For a southern Democrat like Edwards, the most loaded question usually came from rank and file union members. It was about repealing the anti-union Taft-Hartley Act, specifically its section 14 (b), which allowed states to ban union shops.

When Taft-Hartley became the law of the land in 1948, southern state legislatures dominated by business interests had sought to weaken unions and suppress wages by enacting right-to-work (for less) bills. The legislation was hated by trade unionists for two reasons—they made organizing a union much more difficult, and they deprived unions of the dues revenue needed to fully represent all the workers as required by law.

Southern Democrats knew how their local business communities would react if they supported the repeal of Taft Hartley. They also knew how fraught their relationship with unions would be if they came right out and said they opposed the repeal of Taft Hartley. Caught between a rock and their own ambitions, southern presidential candidates danced around the issue. Jimmy Carter said he would sign the legislation if it reached his desk knowing full well that Georgia's two senators would never ever vote for cloture or even consider voting for repeal.

John Edwards, when asked, would interrupt the questioner and filibuster with an answer that applauded all that unions had done, all that he had worked with unions to do and all they hoped to do in the future. Seldom was the follow-up question asked. So, as Labor Day approached in 2007, Senator Edwards was the odds-on favorite to win the endorsement of ten large unions, including my own union—the Machinists.

The Machinists hosted its "Conversation with the Candidates" in Orlando, Florida, in late August 2007. Moderated by CBS correspondent

Erin Moriarty, three Democratic and one Republican presidential candidates were scheduled for one-on-one, 90-minute chats.

Senators John Edwards asked to go first. Ohio Congressman Dennis Kucinich went next. The following day Secretary Hillary Clinton led off and former Arkansas Governor Mike Huckabee followed. Each appeared on the stage separately and was greeted warmly by the 800 local union leaders and international union staff in the audience. The conversations were closed to the press.

The IAM Executive Council wanted to make a dual endorsement— one for their Democratic members and one for their Republican members. And, as Mike Huckabee was the only GOP candidate with the guts to appear before a live labor audience, he was virtually assured of an endorsement.

John Edwards thought so as well.

After touching on Edwards' *Two Americas* theme, the moderator began to ask about his position on the right-to-work legislation. Edwards, predictably, jumped ahead of the question and started answering about his long-standing support for organized labor.

A Phi Beta Kappa member with a law degree from Ohio State University and three decades as a CBS correspondent covering the Gulf War, breaking news stories and murder trials, Moriarty let him run with his answer. When Edwards finished, she followed up simply with, "Senator Edwards, specifically, would repeal of Taft-Hartley section 14(b) be a top priority in your first hundred days? Yes or no?"

Senator Edwards hemmed and hawed but he never said yes. IAM's International President Tom Buffenbarger and the more astute members of this mostly pro-Edwards audience took note.

The remainder of the conversation with Edwards went exceedingly well. The senator from North Carolina left the stage to a standing ovation and headed for a fundraiser across town. He and his staff were certain they had just nailed down the Machinists' endorsement, an endorsement that would trigger a domino effect over the long Labor Day weekend as ten major labor unions announced that they, too, were endorsing John Edwards for president.

Edwards' speedy exit meant that IAM's Executive Council never got a chance to meet with the candidate informally. So his answer on repealing right-to-work hung as a dark cloud over his candidacy, as least as far as Tom Buffenbarger was concerned.

The next day, Ms. Moriarty grilled Hillary Clinton. The moderator hit many of the same issues, including repeal of Taft-Hartley and her support for NAFTA. Senator Clinton did not bat an eye on 14 (b) and agreed she would work to repeal it. Her answer on the North American Free Trade Agreement left open the possibility of sunsetting the treaty if a thorough review determined that it continued to harm American workers.

Clinton's reception was warm but not enthusiastic. After working the rope line until the last Machinists leader had a chance to be photographed with her, Senator Clinton headed to a small reception with select members of the audience. There she was challenged again on NAFTA by an obnoxious Machinist from Canada and an even more obnoxious Edwards' supporter. The former first lady took it in stride.

At one point, her campaign's labor coordinator pulled Hillary Clinton out into the hallway to meet with Tom Buffenbarger one-on-one. The conversation had been scripted by Howard Paster, a senior advisor for the Clinton campaign, for maximum impact. She explicitly asked for the Machinists Union endorsement, said she couldn't go into Labor Day without a single major union endorsement and would never forget that the Machinists had helped her when she most needed it. Buffenbarger agreed to do whatever it took to win her the endorsement. And he did.

That evening, working closely with Transportation Vice President Robert Roach, Jr., Buffenbarger lined up the entire IAM Executive Council save one member to endorse Hillary Clinton. He then instructed his colleagues to work with their staffs to see that the endorsement vote, which was being conducted by computers in the conference center's lobby, reflected the full membership's view.

Prior to the national staff meeting, a membership survey by the union's pollster and an online survey had been conducted. Both showed that Hillary Clinton was the membership's preferred presidential candidate, but narrowly so. The tabulation of those voting in Orlando, however, showed both an overwhelming support for Edwards and an unusually high number declining to vote.

Rather than simply averaging the poll results, the online survey results and the staff's vote tally, I suggested that the non-voting staff members be treated as exactly that, non-voting members. That lowered Edwards' percentage among the staff dramatically and more than enough to swing the average of the three surveys in Hillary Clinton's favor.

The Machinists became the first major union to endorse Hillary Clinton. Its National Staff Conference did do so by acclamation and without a dissenting voice. And the Machinists would stand shoulder to shoulder with her through the long and difficult primary and caucus season—and beyond. For as Tom Buffenbarger reminded the 800 plus local leaders in the audience, the union's close friendship with its past endorsees—Teddy Kennedy, Tom Harkin and Dick Gephardt—lasted long after the polls closed. The relationship forged in the heat of the battle continued on for years and years and, in some instances, for decades.

As the news of the Machinists' endorsement spread, the Edwards campaign went berserk. Other major unions hit the pause button and wondered what the Machinists knew that they did not. The carefully orchestrated series of endorsements of John Edwards over Labor Day weekend fell apart. Only the mineworkers and steelworkers made good on their earlier commitments.

Ironically, even as the Machinists leaders listened to him slip and slide away from answering the Taft Hartley questions, John Edwards was coming to grips with a career-ending crisis of his own making. He was having an extramarital affair with Rielle Hunter, a filmmaker hired to work for his presidential campaign. While rumors would swirl around his campaign in late 2007 and early 2008, the media did not pounce until the summer of 2008. By then, his presidential campaign, marriage and political career lay in ruins.

CHAPTER 3

AMERICA'S STRENGTH: OUR SKILLS, OUR KIDS

I have been unemployed for 19 months now, and I tell you that if I didn't have faith in God I would have committed suicide by now. I have lost my home, my job and my self-esteem. Since I have no vehicle of my own, I have been going to our local library everyday applying for every job online. I have resorted to moving in with my son and daughter-in-law and three granddaughters.

John's Unemployment Story

A month after the Conversations with the Candidates ended, the IAM Communications Department published *Choices*, the cover story for its quarterly journal. The front cover was a close-up of Hillary Clinton, the back cover was one of Mike Huckabee and inside was an 11-page story about the union's dual endorsement. There was also a pointed commentary by Tom Buffenbarger that ended with the line, "It's time to roll up our sleeves and help them secure their party's nominations."

Throughout the fall of 2007, I worked to make the IAM's dual endorsement mean something. Larger unions put boots on the ground in the early states and canvassed their own members. Other smaller unions entered into memorandums of understanding (MOU) with those larger unions, proportionally sharing the costs of events, phone banks, door-to-door canvassing, and, occasionally, television and radio ad campaigns. Most importantly, the MOU for the unions that had endorsed Hillary Clinton allowed them to contact each other's members without running afoul of the federal campaign laws, which restricted spending from union funds for anything but communications with a union's own members.

In states like Iowa, New Hampshire, Nevada and South Carolina, union membership was concentrated in the public sector: the National Education Association (NEA), the American Federation of Teachers (AFT) and the American Federation of State, County and Municipal Employees (AFSCME). And their political operations were first rate.

The Machinists once had a sizable membership in Iowa but its local leadership was sitting on their hands. In New Hampshire, it had a few hundred members. Ditto for Nevada. Only in South Carolina did it have a significant membership concentrated in the transportation sector. Buffenbarger signed on the MOU for the Clinton unions but, since our political operatives who had promoted Edwards at the "Conversation with the Candidates" and were still smarting from the Edwards non-endorsement, there would be few, if any, boots on the ground.

Recognizing the fact that the Machinists' political department, which normally would have been charged with supporting the endorsement, was not going to act, I put together a member contact plan based solely on the resources of the communication department. The membership list was updated for party registration and phone numbers. The dual endorsement would be backed up by oversized postcards and paid phone banks. The post cards and phone calls would be candidate specific, timed to hit in the ten days before each state's primary or caucus, and would continue as long as the candidate remained in the race.[1]

Federal law, at the time, prohibited unions from using their members' dues dollars to communicate with the general public on behalf of, or in opposition to, a candidate. That would change with the Supreme Court's decision in *Citizens United* issued in January 2010. But until then, there was a bright line between paying for advertising and activities involving a political endorsement and an issue campaign where a union advocated for public policy changes. Unions could and often did engage in issue campaigns that did not advocate for or against a candidate.

So, beginning in late November 2007, the Machinists launched a multi-pronged issue campaign called " America's Edge: Our Skills, Our Kids" that urged candidates to re-emphasize technical and vocational education in high schools, expand industrial and manufacturing technology courses in community colleges and create high-tech institutes that focused on twenty-first-century manufacturing technologies.

In a press release announcing the campaign, Buffenbarger complained, "Public investment at the local, state and federal level skews too heavily toward the children who are college bound. We need to provide options for the twenty-four million children who enter high school each decade but do not go on to secure a college degree."

"Blue collar kids need to understand that their innate talents are valued by this society," explained Buffenbarger. "Their career choices cannot be reduced to an either-or proposition. Either get a college degree or accept a minimum wage job—that's not the American way. And creating alternative pathways toward jobs that provide both challenging careers and a solid middle-class livelihood requires greater public investment in technical and vocational education, apprenticeships and community colleges."

The first prong of the campaign was television ads that ran in Iowa, New Hampshire, Nevada and South Carolina. The second prong was an IAM Journal issue entitled *Skills* that, in a unique and unprecedented act of union solidarity, highlighted op-ed pieces penned by Reg Weaver and

Edward J. McElroy, the presidents of NEA and AFT, respectively. The third prong was a four-day, seven-state trek with Kathleen Kennedy Townsend, the former lieutenant governor of Maryland, Tom Vilsack, the former governor of Iowa and Robert Roach, Jr., IAM's general secretary treasurer.

Both the IAM Journal and the fly-around were scheduled for late February, right before the all-important Super Tuesday contests. The issue was joined. Pressure kept building behind the skills initiative until, in mid-July at the Democratic platform committee meeting, language drafted by the AFT and Machinists' policy staffs was made a part of the party's platform.

As the American Edge ads ran in Iowa and New Hampshire, I found myself in Keene, New Hampshire, going door-to-door, something I hadn't done since running for Congress in Columbus, Ohio, in 1984. What they say about the state's snow- and ice-covered roads and the warmth of its people, it's all true. At one house, an elderly gentleman asked us to help take down his Christmas lights and offered us coffee to go. The Granite State, however, was also home to a rare, 180-degree turn by Hillary Clinton's campaign and it began the night before her come-from-behind victory.

CHAPTER 4

SOUTH OF MANCHESTER

... over 17 years with the company, downsized and set up a manufacturing plant in China, that now leaves me looking for a job that is not there for me. I consider myself an experienced worker but it seems that those that possibly would be hiring consider me extinct.

Joann's Unemployment Story

Before heading to New Hampshire, I had called one of Hillary's closest advisors to ask for a favor. Ann Lewis had served in the Clinton White House, at the Democratic National Committee, in Hillary's first senate campaign and on her political action committee. Now she was a senior advisor in a campaign that appeared to be in deep trouble.

Hillary Clinton had come in third in Iowa, trailing John Edwards by a mere two-tenths of a percent and Barack Obama by 8.1 percent. Since losing Iowa, she trailed Obama in almost every poll taken of likely voters in New Hampshire. And all too often the polling suggested a double digit loss in the making.

My requested favor—arranging a dinner for me and my son Christopher with Mark Penn and Mandy Grunwald, who were the campaign's chief strategist and message maven, respectively, somewhere south of Manchester—was neither a personal nor a social one. It was to protect the Machinists' investment in the Clinton candidacy. I was to demand a strategic change in the campaign's direction.

Mark Penn had insisted on a momentum strategy. That meant winning one or two of the first three contests and then winning the four biggest states—California, New York, Massachusetts and New Jersey—by holding primaries on Super Tuesday 2008. Mandy Grunwald, as the campaign's media guru, would be buying ads in those states' extremely costly television markets. If any threesome could force the campaign to do an about face, Penn, Grunwald and Lewis could.

So, Penn and Lewis met me (and my son) at a nondescript steakhouse south of Manchester the night before the New Hampshire primary. Grunwald was a no show.

Before the waiter took our orders, I slid a sheet of paper across the table to Penn. There were no words on it, just a matrix with numbers. And that matrix had not been used since Senator Ted Kennedy had challenged President Jimmy Carter in 1980. As I explained its genesis and connection to the Democratic National Committee's arcane delegate selection rules, Penn's face turned ashen. He understood immediately that his momentum strategy had just gone up in smoke. He was faced with a congressional-district-by-congressional-district fight for delegates.

The matrix laid out the percentage of the vote required to win one additional delegate, a percentage that changed for every congressional district that allowed more than two delegates. As long as a candidate broke through the 15 percent threshold required by the DNC to win any delegates, the marginal increase in votes needed to win one more delegate could be as high as 25 percent. As most CDs had an odd number of delegates, both the Obama and Clinton campaigns could well be fighting for that one delegate margin until one of them threw in the towel.

For example, in a five-delegate congressional district, winning just 30.1 percent of the vote would secure a candidate two delegates and a

two- to three-delegate split. For the trailing candidate to win that third delegate, he or she would have to win an additional 20 percent of the vote—or
50.1 percent—and at an extremely high cost in organization, paid media
and candidate time. In a six-delegate district, getting just 41.8 percent of
the vote would produce three delegates, a three-to-three tie, but it would
take 58.4 percent to win a fourth delegate and break that tie. The cost per
additional delegate became prohibitively expensive, particularly for a campaign that would require a $5-million loan from Hillary Clinton in the
next few weeks.

The upside of the matrix handed to Mark Penn was that, as long
as a campaign competed aggressively, it could expect a very tight race for
pledged delegates. If, however, a campaign failed to compete at all and abandoned a state, then the matrix predicted a blowout in the delegate math.

Notably, that CD-level delegate strategy was one that Barack Obama's
high command had settled on from the start. And that organizational lead
gave him a definite edge. After Iowa and New Hampshire, there were still
more than 432 congressional districts to be contested.[2] Anything could
happen from mid-January to mid-June. So both campaigns settled in for a
long, costly, brutal campaign.

As I came to find out later, the one man most responsible for tweak-
ing the DNC's delegate selection rules since the Kennedy–Carter battle,
Harold Ickes, had been arguing for a similar shift in strategy from within
the Clinton campaign since early fall. So it must have been a shock for him
when, a few days after Clinton's surprising win in New Hampshire, Penn
released a new list of 16 targeted states and, in essence, shifted away from
his momentum strategy.

One problem with this delegate-focused strategy was that the news
media didn't understand it. The rules were too complex to be sexy, so they

reported on what they knew—the polls, the fundraising hauls of each campaign and the daily utterances of the candidates. They were oblivious to the race that actually mattered—the slow, steady accretion of delegates.

The Democratic presidential campaign grew increasingly acrimonious over the next five months. But at the at-large and congressional district level, delegate counts remained within a very narrow range throughout. The matrix predicted a close result, and if a campaign wanted to fight it out to the bitter end, its math dictated a virtual tie.

Large swaths of the country would be won by Hillary Clinton. The urban and older, more diverse suburban counties would be won by Barack Obama. Both candidates would ride massive waves of popular support toward the Democratic Convention in Denver, Colorado. After the last vote was cast and the final caucusgoer was counted, *RealClear Politics*, a political news aggregator, put Obama's total vote at 17,535,458 and Clinton's total vote at 17,493,836, a difference of 41,000 votes out of over 35 million cast.

Even so, a tsunami would overtake the winner. In a backward-looking exercise, the National Bureau of Economic Research (NBER) picked December 2007 as the start of the Great Recession.

None of us gathered that evening was aware that the tectonic plates of American politics were shifting or how destructive the ensuing tidal wave of destruction would be.

CHAPTER 5

COUNTING ON CLINTON

Two weeks ago I had to barter for gas money to get to a job interview an hour away. I'm sitting here relying on family, primarily my 81-year-old Mom to help me pay for necessities.

Lynn's Unemployment Story

The next day Hillary Clinton won the New Hampshire primary, beating Barack Obama by 2.6 percent. In the *RealClear Politics* polling average, Obama had led Clinton by 8.3 points since his Iowa victory. That eleven-point swing came as a shock.

Most pundits pointed to Hillary's tearful encounter with voters in a Portsmouth coffee shop. It was a powerful, revealing moment. But tears alone could not have changed the outcome so decisively. A second hydraulic was at play. New Hampshire's flinty independents were shifting toward the hottest contest in the state—the fight between Arizona Senator John McCain and Mitt Romney, the popular ex-governor of a neighboring state—and away from the overwhelming lead for Obama those polls had captured.

In the Granite State, independent or non-aligned voters could pick their primary. Many often waited until the final weekend, and for any Iowa *bounce* to subside, before deciding where their vote might make a real difference. The shift wasn't driven by philosophy, partisanship, indecision, or even indigestion. They saw upsetting the conventional wisdom as a civic duty. So, thousands of non-aligned voters asked for Republican ballots and McCain ended up winning by 5.5 percent.

One win, however, does not make a president. The battle for the Democratic nomination resumed with a ferocity unseen since the 1980 Kennedy–Carter brawls. Hillary Clinton won the Nevada caucuses; Obama won the South Carolina primary. On Super Tuesday, Obama won 13 states and Clinton won 10 states. And, just as the delegate slating matrix had predicted, the 1,681 at-large and congressional district level delegates split 50-50. Obama won 847 and Clinton won 834, a difference of 13 pledged delegates.

The Clinton campaign's lack of a field organization, the on-the-ground people who identify your supporters and get them to the polls on election day, became all too evident in the mid-February contests and took a real toll on Clinton's chances. Obama won eleven states in row. Their pledged delegates split 289 for Obama to 164 for Clinton. That 125-delegate lead would prove insurmountable, would remain a monument to Obama's delegate strategy and teach an object lesson to those who, like the news media, never understood the rules of the game.

Still the tectonic plates were shifting. While snowstorms blanketed the mountain west and the midwest, a colder, more massive storm kept building. Those WARN notices kept coming: 2,649 in January, 1,837 in February and 1,200 in March. Another troubling index, Extended Mass Layoffs, reported 302,000 separations in the fourth quarter of 2007 and 230,000 separations in the first quarter of 2008. The unemployment lines grew longer; the crest of the tsunami grew taller.

On February 12, as Democrats went to the polls in the District of Columbia, Maryland and Virginia, I wrote a two-page memo for Buffenbarger to be delivered to Hillary Clinton via her personal email account. The memo was titled *Tough Guys Can Get Your Back*. It emphasized,

"Blue collar males are totally invisible in this society. What our guys do—making things with their hands, making machines run—isn't very sexy. It's dirty and gritty and exhausting work. And the work itself vanishes quickly in economic downturns."

"The constant for our guys," Buffenbarger's memo continued, "is JOBS. And a constant fear of losing their jobs. Right now, major metropolitan areas in Ohio like Dayton, Toledo and Cleveland are experiencing 6.5 percent unemployment! That's also true for areas of Wisconsin and Texas."

The memo described a series of surveys the Machinists had conducted of manufacturing states over the past four years. The first poll focused on how blue collar workers faced a vicious downward spiral when laid off. One-quarter had had a job loss in their immediate family in the last two years and three-quarters made far less when they did find a job. The second poll focused on how deeply blue collar males felt the micro-economic pressures build from those macro-economic events. They knew how tough life could get when their cash flow disappeared and their mortgage payments, credit card balances, insurance premiums and utility rates grew. Both polls tested the kinds of messages blue-collar workers would respond to from a candidate.

Buffenbarger's memo ended with: "The tough guys who bend metal, pour concrete, climb poles, make steel and build jets cannot be moved by promises 'to change the world.' They will be drawn to a candidate who recognizes their *real pride* in working with their hands, bringing home the bacon, building something that lasts, giving their kids a fair shot in life and standing tall as Americans.

And they love a good fight.

Blue collar males want a President like Roosevelt, Truman, Kennedy and Johnson who won't back down from the tough fights. Getting universal health care; creating new jobs and new industries; regulating energy, drug and insurance companies and providing skills for our kids—those are fights a real Democratic president relishes. And those are fights you intend to wage and win.

So take that message to where the tough guys work and live. In their plants, bars, bowling alleys, churches, gyms and union halls, these blue collar males are looking for a fighter. Ask them to 'get your back' in the fight for working families."

The memo drew an invitation for Buffenbarger to join the candidate for a private meeting in Wisconsin later that week. A major snowstorm and scheduling snafus altered the timing and location but not the purpose of that one-on-one meeting.

Buffenbarger had been asked to deliver a hard-hitting attack on Barack Obama in a labor rally. So far, no one had laid a glove on the junior senator from Illinois, and Buffenbarger was asked, explicitly, to hammer him on the job losses from the Maytag closing in Galesburg and his passive response to slashed pensions at United Airlines—both had adversely affected Machinists union members.

So I asked Patrick Halley, a former lead advance guy for Clinton during her time as first lady, a consultant to the Machinists on its conventions and a twice-published author, to work with me on drafting the speech. Haley came up with a kick-ass speech aimed at those blue-collar males. I added a few lines about Obama's boxing prowess.

To a basketball auditorium filled with both Clinton's supporters and pro-Obama demonstrators, Buffenbarger drew the distinction between "the Harvard Law Review Editor, the silver tongued orator from Kansas, Hawaii and Illinois, the man in love with the microphone" and "the woman who was hit with the lowest, the cruelest, the meanest attacks that vast right wing conspiracy could deliver."

Buffenbarger then detailed how then-State Senator Barack Obama had spoken to Machinists on Labor Day weekend in 2004. He talked about

how his union was locked in a fight with Maytag to keep them from closing their Galesburg, Illinois, plant and how they planned to lay off 1,600
Machinists and move their jobs to Reynosa, Mexico. He talked about how
Obama had given an uplifting speech and had left those workers floating
on air, filled with hope.

And then, Buffenbarger told this by-now-riotous audience how
Obama had climbed up on that stage having just collected $121,500 in
campaign contributions from the Crown family of Chicago—the majority
shareholders of Maytag, the same company that was sending their jobs to
Mexico to pump up their company's stock price. And he told them how the
Crown family had pocketed over $150 million when Maytag was sold to
Whirlpool a year later.

Calling Obama a terrific shadowboxer, Buffenbarger explained how
when United Airline workers based in Chicago were about to lose their
pensions in the company's self-induced bankruptcy, those Machinists had
asked for Obama's help. He refused. Literally thousands saw their pensions
decimated and their contracts rewritten in the US Bankruptcy Court.

By now, the Obama demonstrators were raging and ranting. So
Buffenbarger twisted the knife a tad:

> "I've got news for all the latte-drinking, Prius-driving,
> Birkenstock-wearing trust fund babies crowding in to hear
> him speak. This guy won't last a round against the Republican
> attack machine. He's a poet, not a fighter.

> Look around you.

> The mortgage crisis is affecting everyone. People are losing
> their homes and even the folks who make their payments
> faithfully are seeing their property values stolen right from
> under their noses.

Unemployment is skyrocketing. Jobs continue to leave our country. Good, solid jobs with the kind of pay check that can support a family. Manufacturing jobs, here in Ohio. Gas costs three bucks a gallon and you practically have to take out a home equity loan to fill you[r] gas tank. Our pensions are looking less robust as the stock market heads south.

This is not time for a poet … the times demand a real fighter! Someone who isn't afraid. Someone who's battle tested. Someone who can take the fight to John McCain and win back the White House. Hillary Clinton is a fighter …

Now, it's time for us to fight for her. Let's let her know 'We've got your back.'"

Clinton's blue-collar supporters in the crowd roared their approval. Obama supporters booed.

To a campaign losing the Wisconsin primary by 19 points and Hawaii's caucuses by 52 points that night, running only on the financial fumes created by Hillary Clinton lending her own campaign $5 million, reeling from a major reshuffling of its senior personnel and busy airing their internal debates in the media, the senior staff's reaction to the speech was sheer disbelief. They were never told that Buffenbarger had been asked to attack Obama. According to the scripts handed out by the advance team at the venue, the campaign was expecting him to introduce AFSCME President Gerry McEntee who would then welcome Hillary Clinton to the stage. Both Buffenbarger and McEntee tossed the scripts away and went with their previously planned remarks.

Buffenbarger's Youngstown speech marked the end of Hillary's string of February losses. He did exactly what he was asked to do—see if Obama could take a punch. Given the Obama campaign's reaction both in the stands and online, the answer was an unequivocal *no*. Within days, the newly reconstituted Clinton campaign took off the kid gloves and started hammering its opponent.

Hillary was doing what Tom Buffenbarger had suggested in his memo, and the results were immediately evident. The working men and women of the Democratic Party had someone who was willing to get in the ring and mix it up on their behalf.

The Machinists were counting on Clinton. And she delivered . . . with wins in the Ohio, Texas, Rhode Island, Pennsylvania, West Virginia, Kentucky, Indiana and Puerto Rico primaries. She lost only the North Carolina and Mississippi primaries and the remaining caucus states. And through mid-June and the last contest, that pledged delegate count grew by another 510 for Clinton and 471 for Obama until it stood at 1,766 for him and 1,639 for her.

The *tough guys* indeed had Hillary's back, but it was not enough.

She lost. He won. Overall, 127 pledged delegates separated them. It was, in the end, that close. In fact, the 2008 contest produced the closest delegate count since 1984 when former Vice President Walter Mondale had defeated Senator Gary Hart by 442 delegates. And Jimmy Carter's 972 delegates lead over Teddy Kennedy was a landslide compared to the Obama–Clinton tally.

CHAPTER 6

RIDING GIANT WAVES

… my daughter who is 20 has quit college to work full time at $10.00 an hour to help support us. I am on unemployment which will run out soon, and am devastated that my daughter will NOT have the opportunity to go to college after all the children I spent years educating have had the chance to do so!

Sandy's Unemployment Story

Every January massive waves surge through Cortes Bank off Southern California. Larger than a tsunami, these gargantuan ocean swells grow as large as a 10-story building and move at speeds approaching 50 miles per hour. An underwater mountain range produces near-perfect tubes, the breaking waves that surfers search for endlessly.

A few intrepid souls, towed behind jet skis, risked horrible wipe-outs to test their mettle against these giant waves. According to the *New York Times*, the surfers "dropped down vertical blue walls 80 feet high or more at perhaps 45 miles per hour—faster than they had ever surfed. They rode cautiously, they said, realizing the consequences of a collision with a 20-pound, lead weighted surfboard, or a harrowing pummeling beneath the dense foam."

Sounds familiar? To me, the 2008 Democratic presidential campaign looked like Cortes Bank tow-in surfing. Senators Obama and Clinton were riding massive waves of voter engagement. By early March, more than 28.3 million Democrats had voted or caucused. Before it was all over, another 7.1 million would add their voices to this chorus of democracy.

Democratic turnout was breaking every record in the books. And by a lot. The year 2008 would see more than triple the number of ballots cast in 1996 when Bill Clinton was nominated. It would more than double the Democratic primary turnouts in 1976, 1980, 1984, 1996, 2000 and 2004. None of those contests even broke 20 million votes. The race between Mike Dukakis, Jesse Jackson and Al Gore in 1988 drew 21.7 million votes.

Halfway to the estimated 70 million votes needed to win the White House, Obama and Clinton were riding waves that deserved respect and awe if not a bit of fear.

For those waves could not be controlled by the candidates, their campaigns, the Democratic National Committee or their GOP opponents. The 24/7 cable news channels focused on the sermons of Obama's pastor Jeremiah Wright or Clinton's dismissal of her strategist and pollster Mark Penn for three or four days. Compared to the Cortes Bank waves, those stories were thunder claps as the lip of the wave hit the water. The constant booming warned that the waves' curl—the tube, as surfers call it—was breaking and the surfers should speed away from the turbulence.

To carry the analogy a bit further, neither candidate could afford to lose focus or relax for even a millisecond. A wipeout at 45 miles per hour is more than humbling; it can be life shattering. Tow-in surfers train to hold their breath for three minutes while tumbling under tons of water. No presidential candidate even thinks about such a sudden, career-ending mishap even though they, too, are engaged in an extreme sport.

Both contestants demonstrated style and grace. Both recovered their balance after some hair-raising turns. Both surfed at the edge of the tube.

And by early March, both Obama and Clinton knew how close they were surfing to each other—fewer than 200 delegates and fewer than 300,000 votes would separate them after the last ballots were cast.[3]

How these two senators finished their historic runs would determine whether or not the winner could, in fact, win the White House. Staying out of one another's and harm's way for more than 100 days was the penultimate test. The ultimate test came as Democrats prepared for their convention in Denver.

Having been an at-large delegate and platform committee member during the 1980 Carter–Kennedy fiasco, I knew how easily a convention could become a self-defeating exercise. Back then the months between the last primaries and the first test votes turned into a titanic confrontation. Every committee appointment in every state, every hearing and meeting and every decision on convention space, speakers and programming became a life and death struggle.

"Reagan's election in 1980 was not preordained," I wrote in a memo to Howard Paster, a senior advisor in the Clinton campaign and an old, dear friend. "It was, however, predicated on the Democratic Party's penchant for self-destruction and self-delusion." That memo, dated March 8, argued for sacrificing tactical advantage to build a strategic edge for the fall, preparing for a war in Denver in order to preserve peace and merging their partisans into a mythic New America. It was written on the heels of Hillary Clinton's victories in Texas and Ohio.

Sacrificing tactical advantage, to me, meant keeping the candidate's focus and that of her major surrogates on the likely Republican nominee, John McCain. "The sharpest arrows in the quiver ought to be aimed at McCain for the next four months; the sharpest needles should be stuck in

Barack but rarely and then only to remind him that the campaign will not let his attacks go unanswered."

Given the speech was crafted a month earlier, that advice seemed hypocritical. The reality was that both campaigns were escalating their attacks and both would have to de-escalate them or risk a repeat of the Carter–Kennedy viciousness. Slowly lowering both the temperature and tempo of attacks would allow both candidates to appeal to the other's core constituencies when the contest was finally decided.

The irony of ironies was that Reagan's peace-through-strength strategy applied to the 2008 Democratic race. Here again, a knowledge of the delegate selection rules was imperative. For in some states, the third- and fourth-stage caucuses were often used to balance the delegation in order to meet gender, racial, ethnic and sexual preference requirements of the party's rules. Additional delegates were to be won IF in-state Clinton supporters were ready to act and think fast. All that was required was quiet preparation by seasoned operatives.

Any lack of preparation, particularly for the rules, credentials and platform committee fights that lay ahead, could blow up in the campaign's face. Inevitably, there would be issues designed to spark floor fights. For example, both Florida and Michigan had broken the Democratic Party's rules by scheduling their primaries before March 1: a convention vote to seat those two delegations would place Barack Obama at a numerical disadvantage. Other equally divisive issues like the Iraq War could be framed in ways to break off blocks of Clinton's support. Yet, each new fight drew a raft of headlines and op-ed pieces. So, knowing ahead of time which fight was worth winning took real thought.

Finally, the campaign had to focus on how the waves of partisans could be merged together in order to win the general election. The memo argued that "the growing power of Senator Clinton's electoral coalition of women, Latinos, blue collar males and seniors is all too obvious. So, too, is the potency of Senator Obama's electoral coalition of Afro-Americans, college students, college educated men and Independents."

"What the two waves lack," I continued, "is an emotional bond that gives them a single identity. That bond CANNOT be a litany of specific issues. It has to be a shared sense ... that we can and will start over, and that THEY define this *New America*."

The contrast between the Old America—an America run by the pale, stale, male and frail—and the New America—an America driven by the vibrant, colorful and powerful forces of change—was soon to become all too real. John McCain secured his party's nomination on March 4, 2008. His last remaining opponent, Ron Paul, refused to call it quits until June 12, 2008. Neither of them could surf worth a damn.

CHAPTER 7

CONVENTION FOR A CHAMPION

Receiving a layoff notice upsets your entire emotional being. The toll on the immediate family is severe. Some friends call to check on you, but unless they have suffered the same fate, they don't understand. Most of them stop calling after a while. Other friends and most of your work acquaintances view you as someone with a plague to be ignored.

Biff's Unemployment Story

Barack Obama and Hillary Clinton kept surfing those gargantuan waves. When all the votes had been cast and all the pledged delegates allotted, Clinton led by 273,000 votes, less than 1 percent of the total 35.3 million votes cast.

As the primaries wound down, members of the Democratic National Committee who had remained neutral throughout moved inexorably into the Obama column. He ended up winning the super delegates by 502 to 251 and hence the nomination. Those un-pledged *super delegates*—senators, members of Congress, governors, state chairs and national committee women and men—delivered the nomination to him on a platter.

And yet, as made explicitly clear in her meetings with her endorsing unions in late May, Clinton had no intention of contesting the convention in Denver. She would not go down the path Ted Kennedy had. Instead she suspended her candidacy on June 7 and endorsed Barack Obama as only she could,

> "The way to continue our fight now, to accomplish the goals for which we stand, is to take our energy, our passion, our strength, and do all we can to help elect Barack Obama, the next president of the United States.
>
> Today, as I suspend my campaign, I congratulate him on the victory he has won and the extraordinary race he has run. I endorse him and throw my full support behind him.
>
> And I ask all of you to join me in working as hard for Barack Obama as you have for me."

There was no bitterness but there were tears in the National Building Museum that day. "As we gather here today in this historic, magnificent building," Senator Clinton reminded supporters, "the fiftieth woman to leave this Earth is orbiting overhead. If we can blast 50 women into space, we will someday launch a woman into the White House."

But her most memorable line, the one that caused even the toughest blue collar guys to tear up was,

> "Although we weren't able to shatter that highest, hardest glass ceiling this time, thanks to you, it's got about 18 million cracks in it, and the light is shining through like never before, filling us all with the hope and the sure knowledge that the path will be a little easier next time."

The Democratic Convention in Denver became a love feast, with open displays of emotion and an outpouring of love and adoration for the nominee and a palpable sense that something historic and dramatic was taking place. Senator Ted Kennedy, who was still recuperating from brain surgery completed barely two months earlier and had then been hospitalized with kidney stones upon his arrival in Denver, made a dramatic appearance.

"As I look ahead, I am strengthened by family and friendship," Kennedy told the overflow crowd who listened with rapt attention and in respectful silence to his every word. "So many of you have been with me in the happiest days and the hardest days. Together we have known success and seen setbacks, victory and defeat."

"But we have never lost our belief that we are all called to a better country and a newer world. And I pledge to you[—]I pledge to you that I will be there next January on the floor of the United States Senate when we begin the great test."

Few noted or even knew how subtly his closing had changed. At the contentious 1980 convention, Teddy ended his speech with "For all those whose cares have been our concern, the work goes on, the cause endures, the hope still lives and the dream shall never die." In Denver, he closed by saying, "the work begins anew. The hope rises again. And the dream lives on." His speech was the dying declaration of a dynasty and a passing of the torch.[4]

And while both Hillary and Bill Clinton wowed the audience inside the hall, it was Barack Obama's speech at Denver's Mile High Stadium that brought out the stars.

"We meet at one of those defining moments—a moment when our nation is at war, our economy is in turmoil and the American promise has been threatened once more.

Tonight, more Americans are out of work and more are working harder for less. More of you have lost your homes and even more are watching your home values plummet. More of you have cars you can't afford to drive, credit card bills you can't afford to pay, and tuition that's beyond your reach.

These challenges are not all of government's making. But the failure to respond is a direct result of a broken politics in Washington and the failed policies of George W. Bush.

America, we are better than these last eight years. We are a better country than this.

And we were."

Alone among the AFL-CIO unions, the Machinists had not yet endorsed "the man in love with a microphone." That endorsement would be made, as it always had been, by the delegates to the IAM's quadrennial grand lodge convention. But there would be a twist.

In an agreement worked out with the Clinton campaign back in the spring, Hillary Clinton would attend the IAM convention in Orlando. Tom Buffenbarger would ask its 1,500 delegates to make her an honorary member, an honor bestowed on an individual only twice in the last 60 years. The union's newest member would then ask the convention to endorse Barack Obama, and, if all went as planned, her motion would be agreed to unanimously.

"You stood with me during that long, hard fought campaign," said an emotional but energized Clinton. "And I want you to know that I will stand with you[,] that I will be your partner and your advocate as we try to change what's going on in this country."

"I believe this country is worth fighting for," Clinton continued. "That's why I got up every morning and did my best to make my case to the American people. We fell a little short, but I will never quit fighting for America, and that's why I am fighting to elect Barack Obama the next president of the United States."

The Machinists were the first union to endorse Hillary Clinton and the last union to leave her side. She had, in the course of twelve months, proven herself to be a *fighting* Machinist. And she left the stage with a lifetime IAM membership card and the union's endorsement of the Obama–Biden ticket.

Two days later, in a two-way video address to the convention, the Democratic presidential nominee and the union's international president traded light-hearted references to *the speech* in Youngstown. Buffenbarger promised to drive the first Prius made in America, one made by unionized workers, all the way from Louisiana to the Obama White House. Obama, in turn, asked Buffenbarger and his union to fight as hard for him as it had for Hillary.

Fifteen hundred delegates laughed at the exchange. And they gave the next president a standing ovation when he said, "Change is a president who's walked on picket lines[,] who doesn't choke on the word 'union' and will finally make the Employee Free Choice Act the law of the land." Their exuberance would not last a week.

Five days later, Lehman Brothers filed for bankruptcy.

CHAPTER 8

MORE GOLD THAN FORT KNOX

I am living with my entire family now, and we are surviving on my unemployment benefits and my uncle's disability check. We all look for work together, but there is none to be had. They've shipped our jobs, let Wall Street print money and swindle us! This has to end! I have worked hard all my life to live my American Dream, and I find it has been stolen, not just from me, but from all of us!

Thomas's Unemployment Story

When Lehman declared bankruptcy, it held assets in excess of $600 billion but no bank would—or could, prudently—lend it a dime. The liquidity crisis, the one that had kept central bankers from Tokyo to Berlin and from London to Washington awake at night for more than 18 months, struck everywhere with a vengeance.

Fannie Mae and Freddie Mac, with $5 trillion in home loans, went from *rescued* to *seized* in a matter of days. HSBC announced a 28 percent fall in its half-year profits. BNP Paribas told its investors they could not take money out. AIG received a $20-billion *lifeline*. The Dow Jones Industrials dropped 2,000 points in a month.

And those WARN notices? 11,300 went out from April 1 through September 30. And the raw unemployment numbers kept rising in those six months. As tracked by Leo Hindery, Jr., who had led four Fortune 1000 companies and now headed up InterMedia Partners, *real* unemployment grew from 12.5 million to 13 million in the second and third quarters of 2007. If the uncounted were included—those who wanted a job but had not looked in a year—16.2 million Americans were already sitting on the sidelines of the American economy.

That was no delayed April Fools' joke.

The American and global economies were caught up in a liquidity vortex that would destroy more than $47 trillion—that's TRILLION with a capital T—in paper wealth within a year.

And yet, like Captain Renault in the film "Casablanca," the financial wizards were "shocked to hear that gambling was going on." No one knew how or why this financial armageddon occurred. Everyone pointed to the subprime mortgage market—risky loans made to low-income borrowers living in rural shanties, urban ghettos and suburban McMansions—and did so with such conviction it had to be true.

But it wasn't.

Black, Latino and white working class neighborhoods across the United States, the supposed epicenters of this subprime lending binge, did not have $47 trillion in assets. Not even in their wildest dreams. News anchors and reporters, however, regurgitated Wall Street's self-serving lie as if they were quoting God herself.

That one lie redirected blame away from the real miscreants. That one lie let the bankers and brokers and insurers and accountants and attorneys and bond rating agencies and even the auto manufacturers off the hook for their sinister and truly significant roles in the largest Ponzi scheme the world had ever seen. That one lie—the destitute did it—enabled corporate America to appear guilt-free as their private jets raced toward Washington to lobby Congress and the Bush administration for bailouts. Over the next few months, America's taxpayers would shell out $2 trillion based on that one lie. A $700-billion bank bailout started that run on US Treasury.

That one lie sped around the globe every day for years. The truth never could catch up. That truth—capital was criminally complicit in its own collapse—was far too controversial for a 30-second campaign ad. That truth was also too complicated to convey in full page newspaper ads or a 750-word op-ed piece.

Fortunately, much truth can be said in jest.

As the Machinists geared up for a three-state, four-day, 14-stop campaign blitz, I had a plywood wall built on top of a flatbed truck. The flatbed served as our mobile stage; the wall was our backdrop and moving billboard. It read, "They got the GOLDMINE. We got the SHAFT."

The Goldmine Tour started with a tiny rally in Paducah, Kentucky. It traveled northeast for an improbable photo op on the highway that passed by Fort Knox, the vault for the US gold reserves. Then it headed to Lexington, Louisville, and Covington, Kentucky, for stops with Bruce Lunsford, the Democrat who was challenging Senate Majority Leader Mitch McConnell. Ending with a stop-by at a fundraiser for the Cincinnati Democrats, it proved to be a crowd-pleaser and provided us with a nice media-driven day in which we garnered headlines and pictures in a number of media markets.

Day two started with a walking tour of the General Electric plant in Evandale, Ohio, where Tom Buffenbarger began his career as a tool and die maker and then a rally at the Painters Union building along I-75 in northern Hamilton County. That event was followed by a roadside rally near the

Armco Steel plant in Middletown, Ohio, with Governors Kathleen Sebelius (D-KS) and Janet Napolitano (D-AZ).

The next day started with a pre-dawn rally in Toledo, Ohio, with members of the United Auto Workers, AFT and AFSCME plus Congresswoman Marcy Kaptur (D-OH). The next stop was a rally in Cleveland, Ohio, and then on to three rallies in Pennsylvania. The first was held during a blizzard in Erie, where only the House Majority Leader Steny Hoyer and a few local candidates braved the storm. Then, in a wild drive to Washington, Pennsylvania, the tour linked up with former President Bill Clinton at a local college. And we—but not Bill Clinton—ended the tour in Moon Township, near the Pittsburgh Airport.

Along this 1,100-mile trek, our mobile billboard "They got the GOLDMINE. We got the SHAFT" drew camera crews and reporters and literally thousands of thumbs ups from commuters and air horn blasts from truck drivers. And hundreds of union members from Kentucky to Ohio to Pennsylvania heard an abridged version of Tom Buffenbarger's speech in Paducah, Kentucky.

His speech humorously focused on that one truth—capital was criminally complicit in its own collapse—began by explaining how we got into the mess.

> "For the last eight years, the Wizards of Wall Street have operated an international Ponzi scheme. They created a blizzard of paper assets—credit swaps, derivatives, collateral debt obligations, structured investment vehicles—that they sold to the Gurus of Global Finance.
>
> The Wizards made a conscious choice to manufacture paper assets rather than manufacture consumer goods. And they loved doing it. It was lucrative. It was easy money.
>
> All they did was staple five reams of paper together and give it a high-minded name like Denali Debt. They stamped it with

their in-house seal of approval and gave it a[n] AAA+ rating. Then the Wizard called one of the Gurus of Global Finance . . . [and] he bought those five reams of worthless paper at a ten percent discount.

Then the Guru sold one of those reams as the First Denali Debt to some idiot in Indonesia who paid full value for that tranche. The Guru collected his fee and dialed up four more idiot savants of the investment world.

In Italy, Iceland, India and Ireland, four more gurus paid a premium price for this . . . priceless piece of mountain high prosperity. And those four Gurus text messaged their clients in Tanzania, Taiwan, Thailand, Tibet, Timor, Togo, Tunisia and Turkey. They offered to sell them a thousand shares of pure mountain air so that they, in turn, could sell slices of Denali Debt to thousands of astute traders."

Buffenbarger's blue collar, working class audiences got the joke. They roared at the stupidity of the gurus and laughed at the venality of the wizards. But they also knew how deadly this Denali debt scheme had become—some had already been laid off from their jobs.

But Buffenbarger kept driving that one truth home: capital was criminally complicit in its own collapse.

"Let me pause here to remind you that no one—not one single wizard, not one single guru, not one single trader and not one single investor—ever laid eyes on that Denali Debt instrument. They NEVER touched that imaginary mountain of prosperity with their bare hands.

So what did the Wizards of Wall Street and the Gurus of Global Finance do next? They did the same damn thing every single business day for the last eight years. Why? Because by creating and trading in such commercial paper—now about as valuable as confetti—they made billions in profits for their firms and millions in bonuses for themselves.

But like all Ponzi schemes, their get-rich-fast machine ground to a halt. After eight years of hyper-greed that stretched across the globe, an estimated 47 trillion dollars—that's TRILLION with a [capital] T—worth of worthless confetti is clogging the drains on Wall Street and the stock exchanges of the world."

Often, when times get tough, humor helps. Gallows humor it's called. But by now, no one was laughing. They knew whose neck would go first into the noose: theirs.

So Buffenbarger turned serious. He talked about how it was time to send in the Feds—the agents of the Federal Bureau of Investigation. How its agents should be swarming over AIG, Morgan Stanley, Fannie Mae, Wachovia and the rest of those failed and failing firms.

And he warned that if that did not happen soon it never would. For he fully expected Treasury Secretary Hank Paulson and Federal Reserve Chairman Ben Bernanke to hold a post-election press conference to announce that "the gold is gone; the gold is gone." Unlike most Americans, he knew that Congress had added $156 billion in *sweeteners* to the $700 billion bank bailout.

Buffenbarger also knew that $856 billion was more than all the gold in Fort Knox and all the gold bars in the New York Federal Reserve Bank, not figuratively but literally, MORE money than ALL of America's gold reserves! And it would not, could not, stop there.

Wall Street got the goldmine, too.

And we got the shaft.

CHAPTER 9

THIRTY MILLION UNEMPLOYED?

I have no propane for the winter… I am a 61-year-old woman and I am out chopping down trees in my yard in order to have firewood for a wood burning stove that we have. My rent is due in a couple days and I don't have it. I cannot sleep. I am becoming severely depressed. I feel the hopelessness that million[s] of others are feeling. Someone please help us!

Linda's Unemployment Story

The presidential election was a foregone conclusion as the calendar turned to November. Barack Obama was leading John McCain by eight points in the polls of likely voter published during the Goldmine Tour. Pundits projected an Electoral College blowout.

The one issue on everyone's mind was the economy, and it was tanking. Since December 2007, nearly three million Americans had been laid off. The human resources folks had put away their pink slips and taken a brief summer vacation but, in September, they got back to work with a vengeance. In total, 163,000 workers were downsized. October would see another 263,000 lose their jobs. Leo Hindery's *real* unemployment number, excluding the uncounted, exceeded 13 million by election day.

Damage from the on-going liquidity crises was spreading. And policy makers, including the Obama transition team and the Democratic congressional leaders, were already wrestling with a stimulus package and an auto manufacturers bailout plan. But no one, not even the so-called experts, really knew how deep the recession would be or how long it would last.

Having been a senate staffer in the deepest, longest recession since World War II, the Reagan Recession of 1981–1982, I knew that unemployment was more than just a number. It was a personal and private tragedy for those who lost their jobs, had their hours cut or gave up looking for a job. What I did not yet know was how massively the American economy had changed in the intervening quarter century.

In a four-page paper circulated to political and policy friends on November 28, I asked an unanswerable question. What do we do if the broadest measures of unemployment exceed 30 million Americans by 2010?

The unemployment report for November, the one issued by the Department of Labor's Bureau of Labor Statistics (BLS) on the first Friday of every month, had said 10.5 million were *officially* unemployed. That was one-third of the number I was projecting for 2010. It was also 2.5 million fewer than Hindery's *real* unemployment number, a disparity that would only grow over time.

My back of the napkin projection was based on the Reagan Recession. It applied the highest percentage of unemployed in 1981–1982 to the significantly larger American workforce expected by 2010. And the paper underscored that point:

"In the 1981–82 Recession, unemployment climbed from 7.8 to 12 million in 18 months. An equivalent percentage increase today would mean unemployment of over 15.3 million Americans.

By December 1982—the high water mark of that recession—the Department of Labor's own statistics for unemployed, involuntary part-time and discouraged workers totaled 20.6 million Americans. Then, the total non-farm workforce was 90.4 million.

If the 1981–82 Recession's rates of increase were applied to the DOL's August 2008 statistics, the number of unemployed, involuntary part-time and discouraged workers would top 28.4 million Americans by February 2010. The non-farm workforce would exceed 136.9 million by then."

In the 2008–2010 timeframe, we would be dealing with a much larger workforce than three and a half decades earlier, 45.5 million larger in 2010 than in 1982. As a result, if the Great Recession was anything like the Reagan Recession, then the number of unemployed would be substantially larger as well. Having one-fifth of our workforce—some 28.4 million men and women—idled was a distinct possibility.

The American economy had changed in the last 36 years. We were less of a manufacturing-based and more of a service-based economy. And the raw numbers not only confirmed but underlined those changes.

"'Goods producing' employment, the hardest hit DOL jobs category in the 1981–82 Recession, had 25.6 million employees at the start of that downturn. Today there are only 21.1 million in the category.

How is that possible? Manufacturing payrolls totaled 20.3 million in July 1981. Today they number 13.4 million. Construction payrolls totaled 4.1 million in July 1981. Today the construction industry accounts for 7.1 million jobs."

The memo predicted that those categories would lose hundreds of thousands of jobs as the recession deepened. But those losses would pale in comparison to the losses in the service sector. Back in 1981, the number of *service producing jobs* outside of retail trade totaled 50.5 million. In 2008, service jobs numbered 100.8 million.

> "While the service sector escaped the 1981–82 Recession almost unscathed, that is unlikely to be the case in this recession. The credit crunch strikes directly at the cash flows of the newer DOL categories of service providers—professional and business, education and health service, leisure and hospitality and government.

> With 100 million jobs at stake, even a modest increase in the number of unemployed complicates America's recovery. Each percentage point increase in joblessness in this   s e c t o r adds one million Americans to rolls of the unemployed."

Beyond the sheer magnitude of the changes in America's workforce, there were also experiential differences that would play out in the lives of the men and women thrown out of work. Qualifying for unemployment benefits was often easier for hourly wage employees than salaried ones, and even then only half of the hourly wage earners would meet the increasingly more stringent requirements legislatures imposed, often at the urging of their state's business leaders, as a way to cut their taxes even in good times.

But if this was to be an inordinately white collar recession, then the experiences of factory workers and construction workers from four decades ago would not be exactly relevant in understanding the crisis at hand. In the 1980s, blue collar workers often found part-time jobs because of their unique skill set. That would not be the case if millions of mid-level managers and sales associates were shown the door. Nor would those college educated workers have experienced the enforced idleness that strikes, supply chain interruptions and minor recessions had forced upon blue collar workers from time to time.

The memo warned that "the coming wave of unemployed Americans will differ in geographic distribution, demographic characteristics and skill sets than those laid off in the early 1980s. So the same old counter-cycli-cal solutions—partially effective as they proved to be nearly four decades ago—may not work very well today."

Having traveled throughout Ohio during the Reagan Recession in the 1980s, I knew from direct experience the toll unemployment took on working families. I had fought through the enforced idleness of trying to find a job after losing a congressional campaign. And my more recent research and travels for the Machinists had exposed me to many, many people who related their painful personal experiences to me. So I urged that the costs of this recession should not be counted solely in terms of federal budget outlays. The unemployed face a daunting, human tragedy. With job losses come unimaginable stresses on individuals and pressures on families. With bankruptcies and foreclosures, the social fabric of neigh-borhoods fray. And there is an incalculable cost in opportunities lost that must be factored in when our economy stalls for 18 or 20 months.

> "While the numbers associated with various economic stim-ulus packages are in the three-to-five-hundred-billion-dollar range, they do not reflect the absolute cost to the American economy of massive and sustained unemployment. Reversing the momentum of a recession is a time[-]consuming, expen-sive proposition. So we might as well make certain that the monies invested will provide a long-term, positive return for America.

> Now is the time to think through a twenty-first-century ver-sion of FDR's Works Progress Administration. That means putting men and women to work on an emergency basis to produce, in FDR's words, 'permanent improvements in living conditions or that creates future new wealth for the nation.'"

The current recession offered a very different challenge than the one I had experienced from the comfort of a well-paying, fairly secure job with a US senator nearly 40 years before. Howard Metzenbaum (D-OH) had been an aggressive advocate for the jobless back then and remained a constant pain-in-the-ass for those who viewed business cycles as a necessary evil to be endured by others.

The memo concluded with two final questions: How will we, as a nation, meet this new challenge? Is anyone willing to ponder that question before we hit 30 million unemployed, involuntary part-time and discouraged workers?

Only a couple of the policy wonks and political hacks—and I mean those as terms of endearment—who received that four-page memo bothered to respond. The rest, like so many others, saw more pessimism than prescience, more pressing problems than solid solutions. And they were not wrong in their assessments.

Nor was I.

December's *official* unemployment shot up by 632,000 to reach 11.1 million. January's went up by 598,000, February's by a whopping 851,000 and March's by 694,000. At the end of the first quarter of 2009, 13.7 million Americans were unemployed. Involuntary part-time and discouraged workers raised the *official* all-in number to 24.95 million.

As a point of comparison, Hindery's *real* unemployment number was 24.8 million through March 2009 and his all-in number was 28.6 million. In the identical time frame and using the *official* numbers as his baseline, Hindery produced a much more accurate picture of unemployment. The spread between the government's *official* and his *real* unemployment kept growing. And the 300 or so senators, members of Congress, their key staffers, reporters and anchors that received Hindery's analysis began to see the Great Recession for what it really was: an economic calamity second only in size to the Great Depression.

The year 2010 was still 21 months away.

My back of the napkin projection did not seem so outlandish as it did only a few months earlier. But the policies produced by the Congress and the Obama transition team remained wholly inadequate to meet the expanding challenge of unemployment. Like folks facing the imminent landfall of a hurricane, they grabbed whatever was still available at the local grocery and hardware stores. Such an off-the-shelf approach, one employed with urgency yet without fully understanding who was or how many were being unemployed, meant that even the best intentioned efforts often went astray.

CHAPTER 10

A SECOND STIMULUS

I want a fighting chance to earn my keep, pay my bills the same month they come in and not have to lie to my son saying that I ate before he got home from school so he doesn't know there wasn't enough for all of us.

Rene's Unemployment Story

As President Barack Obama gave his inaugural address, he looked out over a massive crowd huddled against the subfreezing cold. Stretching from the Capitol to the Washington Monument, more than 1.8 million Americans watched in awe as he sought to reassure the nation.

"Our economy is badly weakened," said the new president, "a consequence of greed and irresponsibility on the part of some, but also our collective failure to make hard choices and prepare the nation for a new age. Homes have been lost, jobs shed, businesses shuttered."

Later in the speech President Obama returned, briefly, to the crises he confronted.

"For everywhere we look, there is work to be done. The state of our economy calls for action, bold and swift. And we will act, not only to create new jobs, but to lay a new foundation for growth. We will build the roads and bridges, the electric grids and digital lines that feed our commerce and bind us together."

He ended his speech reassuring the American people that "In the face of our common dangers, in this winter of our hardship, let us remember these timeless words. With hope and virtue, let us brave once more the icy currents, and endure what storms may come."

It was a stirring speech, one filled with hope, one filled with expectations of change. It was not a policy speech per se but a thematic speech. It was delivered with élan and confidence. And for the 1.8 million Americans shivering on the National Mall that day and the 37.8 million watching from home, President Obama struck exactly the right tone: If we work together, we will succeed.

And his reassurances could not have come at a better time.

Since the November election, 1.7 million Americans had lost their jobs. To put that number in perspective, it was as if every man and woman who had stood on the National Mall and watched the president's inaugural address had been laid off, downsized or fired.

By inauguration day, Obama's transition team led by John Podesta had been working for at least three months on a stimulus package and had been negotiating with congressional leaders. The product of those talks was introduced five days later by Appropriations Committee Chairman David Obey as HR 1, the American Recovery and Reinvestment Act (ARRA).

In the broadest terms, the bill was meant as an $825-billion booster shot for the economy. According to the Washington Post, the House bill added $550 billion to total spending and provided $275 billion in tax cuts. The Congressional Budget Office (CBO) analysis adjusted its overall spend downward to $819 billion, split between goods and services purchased by the government and direct payments to individuals.[5]

While it is hard to quibble with the intent of the legislation or the speed with which it was enacted (with the support of only three Republican senators), the Recovery Act was a classic Keynesian response to a recession—throw money at the problem, almost indiscriminately, in order to increase aggregate demand. And did they ever. Both congressional Democrats and the Obama administration relied on funding off-the-shelf programs. This is why $358 billion went for the purchase of goods and services by the federal government directly or via grants to state and local government. These programs already existed, already were *shovel-ready* and just needed billions more in federal dollars.

The original bill, as scored by the CBO, also provided $119.9 billion for health information technology and temporary increases in Medicaid, and that money went to doctors and hospitals. Another $82.1 billion was allocated for tax credits, and that money went to those who were still working. Notably, the remaining $86.5 billion—or 10.6 percent—went for health insurance for the unemployed and unemployment benefits. Those figures would change, significantly, as the measure moved through Congress. Roughly $32 billion would be cut by the Senate before the bill reached President Obama on February 17 for his signature.

But neither the congressional Democrats who wrote the bill nor the Obama administration who lobbied successfully for its passage understood fully who was being laid off and how long the recession would last. Nobel Prize winning economists like Paul Krugman and Joseph Stiglitz sought to warn them. They argued for a larger stimulus package in late 2008 and early 2009. And within months of enacting the first stimulus, Krugman, Stiglitz and others began arguing for a second stimulus.

I am not an economist. With absolute certitude and conviction, I can say that I do not have the intellectual fire power of two Nobel Prize winners. Not even close. But my experience as a senate staffer in the 1981–82 Reagan Recession, my personal experience of being unemployed for nearly nine months and my back of the napkin projections of 30 million unemployed, involuntary part-time and discouraged workers by 2010 made me realize that a second stimulus was required. And I set about making the micro-economic case, rather than the macro-economic case, for that second infusion of spending.

On February 8, an op-ed piece by Tom Buffenbarger appeared in the Chicago Tribune.[6] It opened ominously by comparing the now global recession to a runaway tractor-trailer. "If the incline is too steep or the load too heavy, downshifting destroys the gearbox. Momentum does the rest. When the rig comes to rest—and it will eventually—the wreckage is found everywhere," Buffenbarger argued. "A second stimulus package is needed," he continued. "Revitalizing America's manufacturing sector must be its highest priority." Here's why.

> "America's trading partners will not buy a trillion dollars in US Treasury notes to finance our recovery as their own economies sink deeper into recession. They've already been burned badly once. Yankee traders sold them toxic debt—the subprime mortgages, credit default swaps and collateralized debt obligations—that triggered this global recession. Selling them more commercial paper stamped 'Made in America' is not a viable option. Our only recourse is to make things other nations will buy. To stimulate our own economic revival, we must renovate our plants, install new machinery and hone the skills of our workforce."

Buffenbarger then called for a 10 percent investment tax credit to rehabilitate and renovate existing manufacturing facilities, a heavily subsidized technical training program for the unemployed that would last for up to two years and an all-of-government effort to fight for manufacturing jobs. Although the op-ed appeared in his hometown paper, President

Obama had moved on to health care reform. He had no intension of, nor any desire to, press for a second stimulus aimed at manufacturing until it was his own job on the line.[7]

At the Machinists' headquarters, the fact that 35,000 of its own members had lost their jobs stimulated a more intense effort to make *Jobs Now* the top priority of the American labor movement. It was a multimedia, multi-month lobbying campaign that would culminate at the AFL-CIO convention in Pittsburgh scheduled for early August 2009.

CHAPTER 11

JOBS NOW!

I'm a plumber. I got hurt on the job ... When I returned I was laid off, being replaced by a temp worker. After all the dedication and almost losing my life for this company, I was let go ... I'm still unemployed at this time and would appreciate any input to what has become of the situation with a man who just wants to do what he does best.

Anthony's Unemployment Story

They say a picture is worth a thousand words. And one can be.

During the spring of 2009, LaToya Egwuekwe, a communications representative who worked for me at the Machinists, used the government's monthly map of unemployment at the county level to create an unbeliev-ably moving presentation called the "Geography of the Recession." In a series of identical, color-coded maps, she demonstrated how each county's unemployment rate grew from December 2007 through May 2009. [8]

Ms. Egwuekwe was a former PBS reporter in Tallahassee who had come to work for the Machinists and was attending graduate school at the George Washington University. She had come up with the idea of a map-in-motion for one of her classes. Not unexpectedly, her map went viral and within months had garnered several million views.

Her multi-color map—yellow for under 3 percent to black for over 10 percent unemployment—showed how the crisis had spread from the east and west coasts and from the nation's major metropolitan areas to engulf, literally, the entire country. The shift from a country filled with bright yellows and reds (4 percent to 5 percent) and enjoying near-full employment to one where purples (7 percent to 9 percent) and blacks dominated was profoundly disturbing.

Egwuekwe's presentation did not include background music. None was needed. The steady month by month darkening of ever larger areas of the country was frightening enough. Every corner of America eventually faced its deepest economic downturn since the Great Depression.

By the summer of 2009, the American Recovery Act had demonstrated its limitations. The jobs *saved* far outnumbered the jobs *created*— as specious as those numbers were. The WARN notices kept coming and would number 23,288 in all of 2009. The *official* BLS monthly unemployment numbers shrank from 851,000 in January to 694,000 in February and 535,000 in March but the percentage of unemployed rose 2.1 points over those three months.

The *real* unemployment number, as projected by Leo Hindery, reached 25.7 million that July. New words and phrases entered into the American vocabulary—jobless and unemployed became synonyms, so did *involuntary part-time* and *underemployed*. And those *discouraged workers* who had not looked for a job for a year, probably, because there were none to be had in their local communities became the *uncounted*. But whatever words were used to describe them, the all-in number reached 29.7 million that July.

Not surprisingly, the IAM Journal's cover story was *Jobs* Now! The article detailed the fear and anxiety the laid-off felt:

"Carol Johnson, a widow and mother of six, lost her job at Hawker Beechcraft. 'I was shocked . . shocked they were going so deep. In my department, they went all the way up to 18 years', she said in reference to her seniority at the plant.

Tina Lopez, an 18-year veteran of the City of Long Beach, was furloughed one day a month for several months then laid off permanently in July. 'I love my job. I never would have expected this. You go for years thinking everything's okay; then suddenly, layoffs started happening. I feel so insecure. And what if you're not old enough to retire, what do you do'?

Kathy Salts, formerly a worker at Bombardier Learjet, worried about health care and her co-workers. 'In my area, there was a young couple. They had three kids. They both got it the same day. It was tough trying to keep their heads high. But the hardest part was losing health care. We're getting older. We have doctors' appointments, but we'll have to cancel them.'"

The article was not all doom and gloom. It also laid out the Machinists Union's suggestions to get the country going again. Stapled inside the magazine were two pre-paid postcards for members to send to House Speaker Nancy Pelosi and Senate Majority Leader Harry Reid. But the Machinists did not stop there.

Earlier in the summer, Tom Buffenbarger had persuaded the general presidents of the Amalgamated Transit Union, International Union of Painters and Allied Trades and United Association of Journeymen and Apprentices of the Plumbing and Pipe Fitting Industry of the United States and Canada to cosponsor a resolution for the upcoming AFL-CIO convention. The resolution was reviewed and amended slightly by the AFL-CIO's legislative committee in the intervening months and submitted to the full convention for consideration on September 14, 2009.

Buffenbarger opened the debate by saying, "Never before have 31 million Americans been idled to this degree. Not in the Reagan Recession of 1981. Not in the Hoover depression of 1929. Only as a result of Bush's financial fiascoes of 2008 have so many become jobless. Thirty-one million American workers, union and non-union alike, are hurting and hurting like they never have before." Given a three-minute time restriction, Buffenbarger made his final points quickly:

"Thirty-one million need jobs now. Thirty-one million Americans need a second stimulus package. A second targeted stimulus package aimed at our manufacturing, construction and transportation sectors can create jobs now.

New policies designed to reignite the engines of growth can generate jobs now. Our resolutions explain how we, as a nation, can do that.

Sisters and brothers, if we are all talk and no action, then those 31 million Americans will be even worse off next year than they are now. Their brightest hope will turn into deep, dark despair. So *jobs now* must become our initiative, our issue, our action agenda and our clarion call.

When we are asked what does labor want? Our answer should be, 'Jobs Now'!"

Buffenbarger's call and response drew the delegates to their feet cheering, according to the stenographers:

"When thousands of teachers and firefighters and letter carriers, government and postal workers and state, county and municipal employees are furloughed, even for a few days each month, what does labor want?"

(Shouts of 'Jobs Now'!)

"When tens of thousands of plumbers, painters, sheet metal workers, iron workers,

bricklayers and electricians are sitting on the bench in hiring halls, what does labor want?"

(Shouts of 'Jobs Now'!)

"And when service employees and, yes, I said the service employees, laborers, teamsters, food and commercial or farm workers are out of work, what does labor want?'"

(Shouts of 'Jobs Now'!)

"So when 5.7 million Americans who want work and can't find a job, what does labor want?"

(Shouts of 'Jobs Now'!)

After speeches by United Auto Worker's Elizabeth Bunn, United Steel Worker's John Redmond and others, the resolution was adopted by voice vote.

Upstairs from the convention floor, delegates, officers and visitors were given a tour of the *Gallery of the Unemployed*. Reprising Dorothea Lange's photographs from the Great Depression, the Machinists' communications department had sent photographers to six cities. Their black and white shots of the members who had lost their jobs were blown up to produce 3 × 4 foot images, all hung at eye level. Their eyes told their stories better than any video could. Along one wall of the gallery hung a massive color-coded map of unemployment at the county level; the last map of the dozens that LaToya Egwuekwe had used.

The newly elected AFL-CIO President Rich Trumka and its Secretary-Treasurer Liz Shuler stopped by. So did many of the recently elected members of its executive committee. Most of them would be involved in varying degrees with the Machinists' next initiative, the launching of a virtual union of the unemployed.

CHAPTER 12

BUILDING A VIRTUAL UNION

I'm a 99er. I have been out of work since the Tuesday before Thanksgiving of 2008 ... There are a multitude of emotions flowing through me at this point. Fear for my family. Where will we live? I can't live in my car with my two children. I can't feed them from a car, bathe them, dress them. My family is no better off than we are, struggling to get by on a day–to–day basis. They can't take us in, even if they had the space, they can't afford to feed three more people ...

Shannon's Unemployment Story

Each summer, my family vacations on a tiny island in Northern Maine. With a vista dominated by Mount Katahdin, our rustic camp lies in the Pemadumcook Chain of Lakes. Its five connected lakes—Ambajejus, Elbow, Pemadumcook, North Twin and South Twin—cover more than 20,000 acres. It's a place of tranquility and beauty, a place about as far as you can get from the tensions and toxicity of Washington, DC.

Fed by the west branch of the Penobscot River, these man-made lakes were meant to carry logs to nearby mills. In 1900, when the Millinocket Mill opened, it was the world's largest paper mill, producing 600 tons per day of newsprint, sulfite pulp and ground wood pulp. Seven years later a sister mill was opened in East Millinocket.

Fast forward to the 1960s and 1970s. By then, the mills employed more than 4,000 workers and generated some of the highest per capita incomes in Maine. These were blue collar jobs available to young men and a few women as well, who graduated from high school and found good-paying jobs with solid benefits. Decades later many retired from those same jobs.

How good were those jobs? According to a Maine Department of Labor report, in 1973 they paid today's equivalent of $68,000 per year. The statewide average then was $38,000! For these two working class communities, the American Dream was built upon millions of acres of trees, free hydropower and 12-hour shifts.

By 2009, both mills were shuttered. Millinocket's mill closed in 2008. The East Millinocket mill was partially shut down the following year. Three thousand millhands found themselves unemployed that summer. Thousands had used up their unemployment benefits, thousands more were dipping into savings just to get by, and a few fortunate souls found jobs by commuting to the coast.[10]

Neither the men and women from the mills nor the local businesses that relied on their paychecks would ever recover fully. For them, there was no refuge from the Great Recession, global competition or the gales of change sweeping through the newspaper and magazine industries. But that bleak future was unimaginable in the summer of 2009.

What my family affectionately calls Rusticators' Island had no electricity and no running water. But it did have a propane refrigerator, a stove and two lamps. The propane tanks (and everything else) were brought across the channel in an old, leaky, aluminum rowboat. Yet the island's small beach and granite boulders were spots where books were devoured, where conversations started and were interrupted by swims and where the economic destruction of the past two years came into sharper focus for me.

Across the channel, the unemployed weren't numbers; they were neighbors. They courageously cobbled together a life after being laid off or downsized. One decided to work part-time at a local bakery where her shift started at 3:30 a.m. Another drove to Mount Dessert Island, a two-hour, 120-mile trip, each week and stayed with his mother-in-law in order to stack shelves and sweep aisles 10 hours a day, four days a week. They lived in nearby, year-round camps but never, ever met.

To them, the huge budget outlays of the American Recovery and Reinvestment Act were not real, but just *Washington talk* and ephemeral promises that might never be kept, and, if kept, they could not bring back those paper mills. To me, all the memos, speeches, videos and op-ed pieces that I had labored over seemed to become meaningless exercises, a meandering flow of words that offered precious little real help to the folks facing the greatest economic crisis since the Great Depression. That realization produced an epiphany: I had to find a way to end the isolation so many jobless Americans felt, give them a way for their voices to be heard in the halls of Congress and create a vehicle for them to drive a distant and indifferent government to act.

On August 27, 2009, having returned from Maine, I gave Tom Buffenbarger a two-page memo. The subject line read, "Ur Union of the Unemployed or UCubed or U3." Even if its list of possible names was completely incoherent, its purpose was clear—let's create a virtual union, one found only in cyberspace.

No bricks, no mortar, no meetings, no dues. UCubed would start off as a community service project of the Machinists. Its costs would be borne by the union's dues-paying members as an act of solidarity with the jobless. Once approved by the IAM Executive Council—and it acted quickly—our web developers took about four months to build out and beta-test the UCubed website.

The most difficult coding task was figuring out how to break the isolation so many jobless Americans felt and let them draw strength from each other. So the math lover in me suggested the concept of cubing—6 times 6 times 6 became 6 cubed—which meant up to 216 new members might communicate with each other. Somehow the developers made it work. And a six-sided cube became UCubed's organizing tool, its logo and its nickname.

When someone entered their zip code and an email address, they launched a cube, a cube with their own photo or icon and five empty sides. As their laid-off friends and family members joined, the remaining sides filled up. If a seventh person joined, the site automatically generated a second cube linked to the first. That process, clunky as it sounds and was even clunkier in reality, was but one element of this unique and useful union.

What was truly unique, back in 2009, was that each person involved in a cube could internally message another member, an entire cube of six people simultaneously, or even a neighborhood of three cubes all at once. As the system was zip code based, the organizing potential of the cube was inordinate . . . if it worked as intended.

By repurposing the Machinists' how-to pamphlets on filing for unemployment benefits, living within a much tighter family budget, writing a skills-focused resume and networking to find a new job, content was created quickly. An existing web-based function allowed activists to e-mail government officials and send letters to the editor. And, in a vain attempt to save the unemployed money, the site linked them to an online shopping mall where users could find deeply discounted clothes, tools and services.

When it finally launched in mid-January 2010, the UCubed website enabled us to post news articles, videos and opinion pieces. Its email list serve gave us a way to reach out to these jobless men and women whenever the Congress, the Obama administration, a governor or a state legislature was about to take action that impacted their lives.

In its first 60 days, UCubed had 1,649 job activists join from 1,400 zip codes. More than 42,000 people had visited the website to view 265,000 pages of content. By mid-April, it was up to 2,000 activists in 1,700 zip codes. The number of visitors steadily increased and page views of the website climbed in lockstep. One reporter called it "an ingenious grassroots union".[11]

But what struck me at the time was that, in the first 90 days, our job activists had sent 16,000 e-mails to the Congress, 10,000 of them supporting a long-term extension of unemployment benefits. Another 3,500 signed on to a 'Throw The Bum Out' petition to Senator Jim Bunning (R-KY), a former major league pitcher who had filibustered a 30-day extension of unemployment benefits.

From reading their comments on various posts, I knew just how angry and frustrated our job activists were. And I knew time was running out for them, their families and the politicians who kept saying "jobs, jobs, jobs" but did zip, zip, zip.

CHAPTER 13

TIME IS RUNNING OUT

Typical Michigan story, lost everything ... I now live in one room. Have no income, turned down for food card. Lucky I get side jobs from time to time but I have kids in college, so anything extra scrounged goes to them ... At 51 years old and no huge degree and no great contacts, I wonder if I will work a regular job ever again.

Chuck's Unemployment Story

What drove the UCubed growth spurt was favorable press. Bloggers at *Alternet, Daily Kos, Common Dreams, Democratic Underground, Iowa Blog* and *Labor Talk* pushed the concept to their readers. Profiles in the *Congressional Quarterly, Chatterbox* and *In These Times* helped build credibility. Even slightly negative stories in *The Nation* and *TechPresident* brought more eyeballs to the UCubed website.

And yet, our most valuable resource was the *Huffington Post*. It welcomed opinionated writers, paid them nothing, but provided a platform that reached an ever-expanding audience. So, during 2010, I wrote and published ten articles that focused on the voting power of the unemployed and their anger-driven politics.

That first article "In Politics, It's All About Timing, and Democratic Governors Could Use Some" set both the tone and the themes that UCubed would hammer for the next six years.[12] The piece began with the cross pressures Democratic candidates would face.

"For Democratic gubernatorial candidates, time is running out. And two uncontrollable forces are making their political lives exceedingly perilous.

First, they face an evaporating electorate. The 2008 presidential election set the high water mark for voter participation. This year's midterm elections, however, will likely see voter participation recede to 2006 levels or even lower.

In crucial gubernatorial races, turnout will be 25 to 45 percent lower this year than in 2008, with the drop-off most precipitous among independents and loosely-aligned partisan voters.

With fewer *swing voters* to appeal to, gubernatorial candidates of both parties will be forced to energize their base vote. And that's where the second force—persistent and pervasive unemployment—paints a big red target on the backs of Democratic gubernatorial candidates."

But it was the sheer magnitude of the unemployed in each state that would drive their politics. The numbers in May 2010 were staggering.

"State and regional unemployment statistics lag behind the national numbers by two months. But the Bureau of Labor Statistics' January 2010 jobless numbers for eight key political states are depressing, truly depressing: Michigan's 14.3% official unemployment rate translates to 693,200 jobless residents, Illinois's rate is at 11.3% with 744,800 looking for work, Ohio is at 10.8% with 640,800 unemployed, Tennessee is at 10.7% with 322,200 residents laid off, and Wisconsin's 8.7% rate still leaves 258,200 of the state's voting age adults without a job. In

Republican toss-up states, California has 2.27 million unemployed and a 12.5% official unemployment rate. Florida has 11
million jobless residents and an 11.9% rate. And Nevada tops
both states with a 13% rate and 178,500 out of work."

I then reminded readers those were the *official* unemployment rates.
The BLS numbers quoted throughout the article represented *only half the
real unemployment*. They excluded those who are working part-time invol-
untarily, the marginally attached and those who have looked for a job in
the last year but could not find one. Nationwide they added 15 million
Americans to the pool of jobless residents.

But the Great Recession was not an equal opportunity un-employer.
It hit key Democratic enclaves harder.

"In large metropolitan areas - the traditional Democratic
base - residents are facing Depression-level official numbers.
The Detroit area has a 15.3% unemployment rate. Chicago is
at 11.1% while Memphis is at 10.6%. Cleveland, Columbus
and Cincinnati are between 9.0 and 9.9% and Milwaukee is
at 8.6%."

Again, these were just the *official* numbers. Doubling those rates
provided a more realistic picture of the size and scope of the problem facing Democratic incumbents, candidates and challengers. In our
nation's minority and immigrant communities, real unemployment rates
approached 50 percent.

Democratic gubernatorial candidates were—and had been—
on notice that the jobless were fed up with the White House and the
Democratically controlled Congress. They felt ignored. They felt helpless.
And they felt that the Democrat's jobs bills were no match for the pain
being inflicted on the nearly 30 million Americans effectively idled by
the Great Recession. So the piece closed with a warning, a warning most
Democrats blithely ignored.

"Losing the Virginia and New Jersey governor's races—and then the Massachusetts Senate race—should have galvanized Democrats at both ends of Pennsylvania Avenue to action. But this 0-for-3 streak did not—instead, they went back to bickering over health care reform while giving only lip service to 'jobs, jobs, jobs…'

So in November when the question turns to what have you done for me lately, the jobless may have a ready answer: Hardly a darn thing!

And if they do, then as for our Democratic gubernatorial hopefuls, it could be, 'Katy, bar the door'!"

Six months later, those ignored, helpless Americans flipped 12 gubernatorial mansions from Democratic to Republican control. Even Katy couldn't bar that door fast enough.

CHAPTER 14

HIRE US, AMERICA

I am a single mother of two... I am desperate. Really wanna die. I had to send my kids to their first day of school with no supplies or school clothes. I understand that everyone is hit hard but is it too much to ask someone to reach out and say, "I'll help you"? ... I would sell myself for the help I need to keep a roof over my head ... Please someone ... Help me, help us. I am terrified. God knows I am a good person, but this situation is making me wanna die.

Teresha's Unemployed Story

Dissatisfied with the paucity of policy options being considered by the White House and Congress, UCubed engaged its jobs activists in an unprecedented online policy development process. On April 15, 2010—Tax Day—we e-mailed everyone a draft 16-point emergency action plan called *Hire Us, America* and asked for their reactions, additions and comments.

Hundreds of e-mails flowed in from around the country. The unemployed, better than most, knew what they needed, and they were not bashful in offering up their ideas. So, that 16-point draft grew into a 21-point plan almost overnight. And then, using the new SurveyMonkey survey tool, those activists were asked to vote on each provision of the revised plan. Many did.

The final *Hire Us, America* plan went far beyond a redress of grievances. It described an America coming to grips with the deepest economic downturn since the Great Depression. Borrowing from the successful programs initiated by Franklin Delano Roosevelt and inventing new proposals to meet the realities of the twenty-first century, the plan gave the powers-that-be a full range of options to end the Great Recession.

The plan was published online, drew the attention of *Daily Kos* and other progressive blogs and was submitted as testimony to the House Subcommittee on Income Security and Family Support of the House Ways and Means Committee. It is reproduced below in its entirety:

Hire Us, America!

1.   Create a Works Progress Administration (WPA) style jobs program and hire the jobless in the public sector. History has proven that in times of widespread economic hardship, when the private sector is unable to hire, it is up to the public sector to jumpstart employment. A twenty-first-century WPA, similar to the President Franklin D. Roosevelt program during the Great Depression, would help get Americans back to work immediately. There's work to be done. The federal government should hire jobless Americans to restore our crumbling urban infrastructure; renovate factories and install new equipment; provide much needed community services in education, public safety, childcare and health care and improve our transportation grid.

2.   Craft a national industrial policy. Much of the current decline in jobs and the US economy can be attributed to decades of failed policies that have governed the US manufacturing sector. The outsourcing of American jobs and bad US trade policies have stifled our middle class and compromised our nation's ability to compete in the twenty-first-century economy.

A recovery without a concerted investment in US manufacturing is no recovery at all. Congress must craft a comprehensive national industrial policy in order to reverse the mistakes of the past, restore the production of American-made goods, get Americans back to work, jumpstart our economy and secure economic prosperity for our nation's future.

3. Discourage outsourcing of American jobs. Allowing US companies to receive tax benefits for sending jobs overseas at a time when over 31 million Americans are either unemployed or underemployed because they can't find full-time work is cruel and unusual punishment. Yet, this atrocity—the exodus of US production and jobs to other parts of the globe—has been going on for decades. Its effects are being felt more now than ever before as the dream of economic security and prosperity slips further away for more and more Americans. Policy changes to discourage outsourcing are a prerequisite to a real US recovery and must be enacted immediately.

4. Renegotiate all trade agreements, beginning with NAFTA. Touted as a key to raising North American living standards, so called "free trade" deals like NAFTA have done quite the opposite. They've created the worst polarization of wealth since the 1920s as multinational corporations have shifted production to areas where wages are low, worker rights nearly nonexistent, and little regard is paid to the environment. A revitalization of US jobs and our nation's hiring cycle requires the U.S to withdraw from NAFTA and all other trade agreements at once.

5. Stop China's unfair currency manipulation. Beijing's policy of holding the value of its currency down to give China an edge in export markets is fueling our record trade deficit, while at the same time stifling US job growth. Experts argue China's currency manipulation has displaced as many as 3 million US jobs. The US must put an end to this injustice by formally citing China for currency manipulation, leveling the playing field by levying a tax on Chinese imports, and adopting a much tougher trade policy.

6.   Enact strong an enforceable "Buy American" legislation. To maintain our manufacturing capability and the millions of jobs that go with it, America must prime the manufacturing pump. We must buy our own products. We cannot expect to restart our major industries and our economy without giving them the business, literally. US taxpayer money should benefit US taxpayers. Strong, enforceable "Buy American" legislation must be a part of the US recovery strategy.

7.   Provide investment tax credits for businesses to modernize their plants and purchase new machinery. A 10 percent investment tax credit for the rehabilitation and renovation of existing manufacturing facilities could pump billions of dollars into modernizing America's plants. With an additional investment tax credit for new equipment, businesses could retool their factories. If these two investment tax credits could be banked to offset future profits, millions of new jobs would be created.

8.   Increase aid to states, counties and municipalities in order to restore and/or maintain vital services. Many communities have laid off, furloughed and cut back on hiring teachers, police, firefighters, childcare providers, emergency health care providers and transportation personnel due to the poor economy. Providing local governments with the financial means to restore and/or maintain these critical services will prevent local tax increases, increase employment in the community and stimulate local businesses as families start spending again.

9.   Pool a portion of the Obama Cabinet's discretionary funds and use those monies to create emergency-job-creation programs in communities with the highest levels of unemployment. Each year, Congress appropriates billions of dollars that can be used at the various cabinet secretaries' discretion. And each year, billions of dollars are spent helter skelter in the final months of the fiscal year. So, rather than throwing money at government contractors, a portion of those discretionary funds should be dedicated to putting Americans back to work. Under the direction and supervision of

the White House, these pooled discretionary funds could jump-start local job creation.

10. Make Wall Street pay back Main Street through the enactment of a financial transactions tax [act]. Taxing financial transactions on Wall Street only makes sense. After all, it was Wall Street and its affection for reckless deals, which broke the economy in the first place. Economists argue a small fee on the sale or transfer of stocks, bonds and other financial assets could generate as much as $100 to $150 billion a year. The money could then be used to pay for temporary aid to states, serve as hiring incentives for public- and private-sector employers and fund infrastructure projects.

11. Build a revitalized, green economy by investing in green jobs. In addition to infrastructure jobs, green jobs will also help to ensure continuous growth and preserve America's economic security. We need to be investing in the kinds of jobs that build and sustain our economy over time. The clean energy sector offers enormous opportunities to do just that, reviving our economy while at the same time helping the US to become a leader in renewable energy and energy efficiency.

12. Provide incentives for skills training and higher education. A plan for moving our country forward and reenergizing our workforce must also include measures for preparing our workforce for the future. Two years of technical training should be offered to both unemployed workers and recent high school graduates free of charge. And, tuition at community colleges, universities and high-tech institutes should be heavily subsidized, just as Roosevelt's GI Bill did after World War II.

13. Extend unemployment insurance benefits. Millions of unemployed Americans, idled in this Great Recession through no fault of their own, depend on unemployment insurance benefits to carry them through. For many, it is the only source of income and means for providing for themselves and their family. With the ranks of long-term joblessness continuing to grow and this Great Recession achieving record depths, it is wrong

to continue stringing the jobless along with temporary benefit extensions. This recession is far from over. Congress must act now to craft a long-term extension and preserve this much-needed lifeline.

14. Add a Tier 5 to unemployment benefit extensions. The recession took many economists and government officials by surprise. And though they knew it was deep, no one expected folks to be out of work for as long as 99 weeks. Yet, thousands of people have been and are. It's safe to say at this point, these former workers are not in a recession, but a depression. Many idled through no fault of their own haven't seen an unemployment check in months. Congress' temporary extensions to date only cover the jobless receiving unemployment benefits for less than 99 weeks (Tier 4 or lower). Workers unemployed for longer than that need help. Congress must add a Tier 5 to all further extensions to cover these long-term unemployed Americans.

15. Extend COBRA and the 65 percent subsidy. COBRA allows millions of Americans to continue receiving health care benefits for a maximum of 18 months after leaving their employer. But in a recession plagued by long-term unemployment, more and more people are finding themselves out of work long after their benefits expire. When passing the health care reform bill, Congress failed to include a measure extending COBRA benefits until 2014, when many of the new, state-run health care exchanges would be in place. In addition, measures to extend a 65 percent government subsidy, which helps millions even afford COBRA coverage, continue to hang in a political purgatory. Without COBRA or the subsidy, many jobless Americans will be left without health care coverage or, worse, forced to forgo coverage in order to feed their family, pay bills and/or keep a roof over their head. A long-term extension of overall COBRA coverage and the 65 percent subsidy would ensure [that] workers and their families are continuously protected.

16. Increase the maximum food stamp benefit amount; expand the income requirement threshold for eligibility to include the jobless and adjust the eligibility requirements to ensure that the long-term unemployed can readily qualify. Food is no longer an everyday expense for millions of Americans who have lost their jobs. In many cases, buying groceries is sometimes weighed against making a rent or mortgage payment, seeking medical care or paying a utility bill. For that reason, millions of jobless Americans have turned to food stamps. But research shows that by the third week, 90 percent of those benefits are gone in the average household. In addition, thousands of jobless Americans, especially those without dependents, have been denied food assistance because they don't meet the income requirements. Even when applying under meager unemployment benefits, many are being told they make too much money and are, therefore, denied help. We need to ensure every unemployed person receives the supplemental nutrition assistance they need to make it through these very long and extremely difficult times.

17. Re-create the Comprehensive Employment and Training Act (CETA) program; target new jobs to employ the structurally unemployed and focus on economically depressed communities. A re-creation of the CETA program will help idled Americans get back to work today, while preparing them for the jobs of tomorrow. Enacted in 1973, CETA trained workers and provided them with jobs in the public sector. The program targeted those with low incomes and the long-term unemployed. It also provided jobs to low-income high school students in the summer. The intent was to provide the unemployed with marketable skills needed to find permanent employment.

18. Permit unemployed Americans to tap their retirement accounts without incurring a 10 percent penalty for early withdrawals. The jobless may have lost their jobs, but their mortgage, bills and financial obligation to their families still exist—in fact, in many cases the cost has gone up. Because they're tight on cash, many are looking to their nest egg to help make up

the difference. In light of the historic financial crisis, federal policy should ensure that unemployed workers needing to tap into their retirement savings earlier than expected aren't penalized for simply trying to keep their head above water today.

19. Re-imagine the Workforce Development Act (WIA) to integrate regional training systems in order to retool America's workforce and transform regional economies. As Congress debates reauthorization of the 1998 WIA, it should consider amending the employment training and vocational development law to promote talent development amongst regions, rather than at the local level. The current system all too often creates silos that, in some cases, result in workers being trained for jobs that do not meet current and future employer and economic needs. By thinking and collaborating across functional and jurisdictional boundaries, workforce development leaders can work to ensure the various stakeholders— employers, economic development and workforce development boards, community colleges and others—create effective approaches to transforming their regional economies and providing high-wage job opportunities for workers.

20. Reinstitute the Civilian Conservation Corps (CCC) and fund conservation projects and improvements in our national and state parks. The CCC was a public works relief program focused on conservation and natural resource development projects during the Great Depression. More than 3 million young men, aged 18 to 24, were put to work on planting trees and constructing parks. The result of their work can be seen in many of today's state parks. Reinstituting a twenty-first-century CCC program for today's unemployed would boost our economy, while at the same time help to improve the environment.

21. Bar employers from using a job applicant's credit rating as a basis for employment. Millions of Americans are finding themselves in a catch-22 in this financial crisis: they have bad credit because they lost their job, and

they can't get a job because they have bad credit. More and more companies have added credit checks to their job screening checklists as a means of assessing an applicant's "character." Truth is there is currently no hard evidence proving one has anything to do with the other, especially when more than 31 million Americans have been kicked out of the job market through no fault of their own. The Equal Employment for All Act, HR 3149, seeks to end employer credit checks. Its enactment would give vulnerable "credit challenged" citizens—students, recent college graduates, low-income families, senior citizens and minorities—an opportunity to rebuild their credit history by getting a job.

Over the course of the next three Congresses, some but not all of the 21 points were enacted into law. The bigger, more costly proposals died ignominious bipartisan deaths in a wave of GOP-sponsored austerity measures, measures predicated on their winning control of the House and Senate and nearly a dozen governors' mansions.

What was most remarkable, however, was the disdain with which the plan was met by Democratic elected officials and their strategists. It was dismissed out-of-hand. After passing the American Recovery and Reinvestment Act in February 2009, the party of FDR saw no reason to do much more for the unemployed, underemployed or uncounted.

Instead, Democratic leaders focused their energies on defending the Patient Protection and Affordable Care Act, soon to be known as Obamacare, which was signed into law three weeks before the *Hire Us, America* plan was published. Democrats were intent on running on that singular achievement all the way to November 2010.

CHAPTER 15

KEYSTONE TO VICTORY

My son-in-law, a union construction worker, was laid off in early 2009 ... He had four children. He began having chest pains at the end of October and felt he could not afford to go to the doctor ... no money. He died November 15, 2010[,] when the aneurysm that was causing the chest pain ruptured while he was driving. Now my grandchildren have no father and my daughter who is also unemployed has lost his UE benefits and is left to manage on her own ...

Elke's Unemployment Story

In the darkest days of the Great Recession, I had a casual conversation with US Senator Bob Casey (D-PA). When our chat turned to the jobless, he cut me off with "the unemployed don't vote."

It was a common misconception among Democrats, and a willful one. Taking their lead from the Obama White House, Democrats saw green shoots sprouting all across the land. As autumn follows summer, they expected to harvest the votes of those employed in a roaring recovery.

Besides, as the jobless didn't vote, why even talk about them? Or *to* them? I disagreed. During the primaries, UCubed had spent tens of thousands of dollars on cable television ads to increase primary turnout among unemployed voters.

Our ads opened with a video of a Phillips screw being drilled into a block of wood while black and white photos of the unemployed flashed in the background. "LAID OFF, DOWN-SIZED, OUT SOURCED" were stamped in red across their chests. As the screech of the drill died away, the announcer said, "Now, we get to turn the screws. We have the power to put America back to work." A graphic with "GO VOTE" filled the screen.

The ads ran in the week before the Pennsylvania and South Carolina primaries, states with 629,000 and 249,000 unemployed citizens, respectively. The edgy messaging was meant to resonate with the working class Democrats who were still looking for work.

How many jobless voters actually went to the polls, however, was never clear. Neither the Pennsylvania nor the South Carolina primary had exit polls. Only the results provided a clue.

In Pennsylvania's senate primary, the winner was Joe Sestak, a former three-star admiral and a sitting congressman. He beat Arlen Specter, the incumbent who had switched parties earlier in the year. Sestak won by 81,000 votes out of a million cast.

In the high unemployment areas in the Keystone State where the UCubed television ads appeared—Center, Cambria, Cumberland, Chester, Dauphin, York, Lancaster and Lackawanna counties—turnout was 6 percent to 12 percent higher than in the last competitive statewide primary between Bob Casey, the son of the recently deceased governor, and Philadelphia Mayor Ed Rendell. Turnout was slightly lower but within 5,000 votes of that 2002 race in Berks, Delaware, Erie, Northampton and Washington counties. Even though nearly 200,000 more Pennsylvanian Democrats voted statewide in 2002 than in 2010, it is impossible to claim credit for the turnout levels in those 13 counties even with thousands of ads hitting the jobless where they lived—in their own dens and living rooms—every day for a week.

But there is one more factor in Pennsylvania to consider that also played out in South Carolina. In both states, turnout in the 2008 Democratic presidential primaries between Obama and Clinton were record-breaking affairs. In Pennsylvanian, it topped 2.3 million, almost 1.3 million more than in 2010. In South Carolina, more than 529,000 Democrats voted in 2008 while only 170,000 did in 2010, a fall off of 359,000 votes. If the unemployed did not vote, as Pennsylvania Senator Casey suggested, then neither did those still working. But both the jobless and those with jobs *were*, by definition, *already registered to vote* having voted in the presidential contests.

And, if UCubed could galvanize them to go vote, their voters were worth something. They could—and they did, as South Carolina proved—make a huge difference in a relatively low turnout contest.

In South Carolina, an unemployed African-American, Alvin Greene, won the Democratic primary by 30,500 votes. His opponent, Vic Rawl, had campaigned aggressively and won among voters using absentee ballots. But Greene, who spent no money, held no campaign events and did not have a website, won decisively among those who voted on election day.

South Carolinians did not vote for Greene over Rawl because of the UCubed ads or the candidates' job status. Given the massive registration efforts of the Clinton and Obama campaigns two years earlier, the results were driven mostly by name recognition. First names and surnames were the only clues many voters had—or needed—to make their decisions in a state riven by racial tensions. But reminding folks that they were getting screwed in the Great Recession was not very difficult when South Carolinians faced an *official* unemployment rate that exceeded 12 percent.

Turnout proved significantly higher in the Palmetto State than in its non-presidential primaries going back two decades. The results there and in the Keystone State spoke volumes. Yet sparse data and anecdotal evidence was useless against the conventional wisdom. Then along came the Census Bureau.

After each election, the US Census Bureau reports on registration and voting. Separate data tables are published providing information on age, race, gender, region, education and employment status. That last category covered the unemployed. In the midterm election of 2006, the last midterm election before the Great Recession struck, the unemployed numbered 5.61 million. About 3 million were registered to vote. Only 1.75 million voted. Less than a third (31.2 percent) of these structurally unemployed Americans went to the polls in November of that year.

By the time of the 2010 midterm elections, which took place near the high water mark of the Great Recession, the number of unemployed citizens had risen to 12.4 million—more than double the census number in 2006. Voter registration rates had also more than doubled but their turnout levels had slipped slightly to 27.4 percent. What a difference 4 years make. According to the Census Bureau, only 1.75 million unemployed citizens voted in 2006 as compared to 3 million in 2010.

And yet, the 2010 exit polls told a far more persuasive story. They reported that 30 percent of *all* voters came from *households that had experienced unemployment* in the prior 2 years. That was three times the *official unemployment rate* of 9.6 percent generated by the US Department of Labor and 13 points higher than the *real* unemployment rate of 16.9 percent that Leo Hindery reported for November 2010.

Those emphasis-added phrases plagued the jobless throughout the Great Recession. More than mere semantics, their definitions drove decisions and decision-makers. Exit polls probed voters from unemployed households. The Census Bureau asked respondents to recall their working status, voter registration and voting behavior from a year earlier. The Bureau of Labor Statistics (BLS) surveyed a panel of 60,000 each month to determine if they were working full-time, part-time, had been laid off or had left the workforce entirely.

UCubed focused on *real* unemployment rate and often relied on the broadest measure of unemployment, U-6, which was compiled from the BLS data. The media used U-3, the *official* and much lower unemployment rate BLS reported on the first Friday of each month. Democratic elected officials and their political consultants managed to ignore both and, owing to a timing quirk, seldom saw even the exit poll crosstabs.

Numbers. Numbers. Numbers.

Former British Prime Minister Benjamin Disraeli once commented, "There are three types of lies: lies, damned lies, and statistics." Well, the economic community was also operating in threes.

Three different sets. Three different policy drivers. Three or more different political calculations. All led to very, very different conclusions about the raw political power of the unemployed.

No matter which set of numbers you used, however, the 2010 election results proved to be disastrous for the unemployed. Officially, the unemployment rate had "edged up to 9.8 percent" that November and "the number of unemployed persons was 15.1 million." [13]

Those two numbers did not arrive until a month after the polls had closed. And the exit poll crosstabs, the ones containing those unemployed household numbers, did not become available until six weeks after the election. By then, the media had moved on.

Those 2010 exit polls reported that unemployed households gave Democratic congressional candidates a slight four-point edge over their Republican opponents. Those nationwide numbers came as cold comfort to Democratic incumbents on the losing side of what President Obama called a shellacking just days after the election.

If 2010 was a wave election, then the unemployed were its riptide. Unseen, unnoticed and unreported, voters from those jobless households dragged 750 Democrats under and drowned them in a sea of their own indifference.

In eight out of nine states where the exit polls asked voters about the unemployed living in their own households, voter responses ranged from 34 percent to 41 percent of the electorate, three to four times the *official* unemployment rate for those states. Those were voters who lived with a jobless person, who saw what that person went through, who watched them become more and more isolated and who knew how little the Democrats had done to put them back to work.

In Pennsylvania, where Senator Bob Casey claimed the unemployed didn't vote, one-third (34 percent) of the turnout came from unemployed households. Its unemployed households split 56 percent to 44 percent for Democratic nominee, Joe Sestak, and Republican, Pat Toomey, who still won by 79,000 votes. Had Sestak appealed directly to unemployed households, fought for the massive jobs programs they so desperately needed and explained how anti-jobless and pro-austerity his Republican opponent was, the outcome might have been far different.

But "shoulda, woulda, coulda," few Democrats aggressively campaigned for the unemployed vote. Only Senators Barbara Boxer (D-CA) and Harry Reid (D-NV) made explicit appeals to the jobless in 2010. They won their races by 16 and 12 points, respectively.

For the Democratic Party whose traditions of fighting for the unemployed dated back to the Great Depression, shunning the jobless proved to be a miscalculation that went well beyond political malpractice. It was an exercise in mass, unassisted suicide.

The unemployed, underemployed and uncounted would be the key-stones to victory or defeat in the years ahead. And the Democrats' blithe indifference to them would be long remembered in those jobless house-holds, those that comprised one-third of the electorate, those that split their congressional candidates 50 percent to 46 percent.

CHAPTER 16

A VENDETTA AGAINST JOBLESS AMERICANS

I feel hopeless. I feel useless. I feel angry. Here I am, having improved myself, to make myself worthy, and, because of my age, no one is willing to hire me. My American Dream is shattered, as it was shattered for my father in 1984 when he lost his factory job after 17 years. I feel scared ...

Scot's Unemployment Story

Prescience, particularly in politics, is a curse, not a blessing. By May 2010 it was clear to me that the unemployed believed that President Obama had turned his back on them. They saw congressional Democrats, like Senator Bob Casey, as impediments to their return to work. Their comments on posts by UCubed on its Facebook page grew angrier and angrier.

On the far right, media *personalities* like Glenn Beck and Rush Limbaugh stoked a sense of anger *against* the unemployed. Congressional Republicans, intent on making Barack Obama a one-term president and seeing a pathway to power, browbeat the jobless.

Republican lawmakers, playing to the cheap seats, telegraphed their deep disdain for the unemployed. Jim Bunning (KY) did so with his one-man filibuster against extended unemployment. John Kyl (TX) suggested unemployment acted as "a disincentive for them to seek new work." Orrin Hatch (UT) felt the jobless should be drug tested in order to qualify for unemployment benefits. And Dean Heller (NV) used the word "hobos" to demean those on unemployment.

Republican attacks on America's jobless were not random acts of meanness. Nor were they the ravings of a lunatic fringe. They were hostile acts in a partisan strategy. By attacking the powerless, GOP lawmakers aligned their party with the powerful. By assailing the jobless, they expected to win control of the Senate and, ultimately, win back the White House.

Then they backed up their words with their votes.

Starting with their vehement opposition to the American Recovery and Reinvestment Act (ARRA), House and Senate Republicans cast 1,477 votes against that jobs bill and 44 votes in its support! Thirty-five of those 44 votes opposed motions to recommit. So, the single largest job creation bill in American history drew but nine GOP votes—three each from Senators Olympia Snowe, Susan Collins and Arlen Specter. And that was it—only nine votes in support of the jobless out of 1,521 votes cast by the Grand Old Party of Calvin Coolidge and Herbert Hoover on the ARRA.

An identical pattern appeared on the appropriations bill for the Department of Commerce and the Justice Department for Fiscal Year 2010 that dealt, in part, with unemployment insurance and COBRA. Across 33 roll call votes conducted in both chambers, Republicans cast 4,191 votes in opposition and only 239 votes in support of the measure. The GOP's vendetta was unrelenting.

When Democrats sought a two-month extension of unemployment benefits and the COBRA subsidy in April 2010, the GOP, in a successful attempt to throw sand in the gears of progress, forced eight procedural votes in the Senate. Minority Leader Mitch McConnell (R-KY) caused his caucus to cast 323 votes against helping the unemployed. Only three Republican Senators cast votes to aid the jobless.

Not surprisingly, when a five-month extension of benefits for the unemployed moved through the Congress, the GOP assault grew even more vicious and lopsided. The Tax Extender Act, which was being considered in mid-June 2010, drew 1,199 GOP votes against helping the jobless. Just 35 GOP votes were recorded for the jobless.

On all four measures—each a vital lifeline for the unemployed—Republicans in both chambers cast 7,291 votes against the jobless and only 371 to help them. Democrats cast 10,440 votes to help the jobless and 568 votes to harm them. The contrast between the two parties could not have been more striking.

Not once, but on 65 separate roll call votes, did the Grand Old Party stick a stiletto in the back of America's unemployed, underemployed and uncounted. Those repeated thrusts, crimes not of passion but of cold-blooded revenge, were payback. Republican lawmakers knew that the surge voters of 2008 that had elected Barack Obama the forty-fourth president— the blue collar workers without a high school diploma, African-Americans, Latinos, union members and college students—were experiencing the highest rates of unemployment of any demographic group. So with each vote they cast, the GOP gave that stiletto a sharp twist.

Democrats, who should have come to the defense of the jobless out of a keen sense of self-preservation, if not solidarity, declined to make the case. Republican attacks on those surge voters, the voters who elected Barack Obama, went unanswered. As a result, the men and women who felt those knives twist, who felt hopeless and defenseless, who needed a champion now more than at any other point in their lives also felt completely abandoned by the so-called party of the little guy.

Instead of pointing out who had voted against the stimulus, who had held their unemployment benefits hostage and who had voted against the COBRA health insurance subsidies, Democrats were drawn into a spurious and furious debate over Obamacare. Republicans described it as "the job-killing ObamaCare law." They claimed it would "result in a government takeover of health care." And they "pledged to repeal it, and replace it with common-sense reforms."

From the Oval Office to the Majority Leader's Office to the Speakers' Office, Democrats raced to rebut those attacks. Their campaigns ads focused on the 85 percent of Americans still employed who could afford to buy health insurance or whose employers did, whose pre-existing conditions would not now bar them from being insured and whose adult children (up to age 26) would be covered under their parent's policy. But those Americans lucky enough to be employed during the Great Recession were not the problem; they outnumbered the unemployed by six to one; and, with good reason, they were enjoying life to the fullest.

So Democratic candidates and their strategists, convinced that the unemployed would not vote in the midterm elections, focused millions of dollars in television ads on the narrowest slice of *persuadable voters*— the *undecideds* who would vote on election day. And they consciously and cravenly ignored the unemployed.

Meanwhile, some 31 million jobless Americans just seethed and waited for the polls to open.

CHAPTER 17

THE LAST (SAD) LAUGHS

I am currently unemployed and my fight is different from many others. I devoted the majority of my adult life to raising my kids. I learned (not college learned) MANY skills during the 25 years that I spent taking care of my three from ages 0 to 18. These skills are not looked at by employers, well basically they are LAUGHED at by employers.

Cheryl's Unemployed Story

Back in June 2011, the *Huffington Post* had accepted another one of my provocative posts. This one focused on another mind-numbing set of numbers: non-farm payrolls. The BLS had tracked their monthly rise and fall since 1939. For those seven decades, its non-farm payroll table offered a quick summary of America's actual, annual job creation.

The BLS table also provided a strong indicator of what might be possible in the future. America's best three-year job creation total was 10.3 million that occurred during the Clinton administration from 1997 to 1999. Our second best effort produced 9.4 million jobs between 2004 and 2006. The third best performance was 7.7 million jobs in the years 1984 to 1986. Sadly, none of those record-breaking surges in job creation came even close to the job losses in the Great Recession.

Since December 2007, non-farm payrolls had declined by 11.2 million. Replacing those jobs—and adding the 140,000 a month needed in order to keep pace with the natural growth in the labor force—would require a three-year burst of over 16 million jobs. The magnitude of that challenge ought to have concentrated the best minds in the country. Instead the exact opposite occurred.

"The White House and Congress," I argued, "seem wildly disconnected from the jobs crisis, perhaps because they take so much time aiming a strobe light on health care reform, Iraqi elections, a new START treaty, financial industry reform, climate change, an amended No Child Left Behind, Afghanistan and a balanced budget." The best minds were dispersed, distracted and devoted to their own agendas.

This glaringly obvious sentiment that no one seemed to give a damn about the men and women looking for work would have severe consequences:

"Like the 'unemployables' of the Great Depression before FDR came along, America's jobless today face the cruelest of choices: hunger, homelessness and declining health. And their anxiety and anger are growing even as their hope fades.

But the jobless are not completely destitute in a democracy. They still own their votes, which can be 'spent' on election days or not. And if the BLS total non-farm payroll history is any indication, the jobless will have at least three election cycles—2010, 2012 and 2014—to spend those votes, and then, as embittered as they may be, theirs will be the 'last (sad) laughs.'"

Never had I penned words so prescient or so pessimistic. And yet, as pessimistic as they were, I was still one election cycle shy of a full house. The last (saddest) laughs would come in November 2016.

No political outcome is ever foreordained. There's always a chance that an October surprise occurs to confound the conventional wisdom. Unfortunately, the surprise in 2010 was that there wasn't one.

During the month of September, I traveled to nine states, three as part of the Machinists' Goldmine Tour and six more states as part of the Painters Union's cross-country JOBS tour.[14] I listened to more than 200 campaign speeches. In all those speeches by Democratic candidates for the US Senate, Congress or governor, there were only *two* passing references to President Obama. After two years, he was so unpopular Democratic candidates ran away from him. Plus I saw a complete disconnect between Democratic politicians and their audiences. The most rousing close to a speech that I heard was by an Oregon candidate who urged his labor audience to "give Congress heck."

Far too polite for my taste, but then Heck was his last name. Not surprisingly, he lost.

What struck me most, however, were the candidates' bloodless appeals to the jobless. They knew the *official* unemployment numbers by heart. But their speeches were devoid of any passion—not a phrase about the pain, anxiety or isolation that the jobless felt passed their lips. Their aloof and cerebral approach mimicked their president's public personae. Imitation may be the finest form of flattery but, in this instance, it chilled every audience.

In 2010, the *red meat* and *red faced* speeches belonged to the Tea Party's activists and candidates. From their tricornered hats to their yellow "Don't Tread On Me" flags, they thought of themselves as kin to the patriots who had dumped boxes of tea into Boston Harbor before the American Revolution. And their rhetoric was as inflammatory as the Democrats' rhetoric was frosty.

Rand Paul, who won a barely contested GOP primary in Kentucky,[15] was an example of the Tea Party's pyrotechnical approach. His campaign events, according to the *Washington Post*, "were feisty affairs heavy on a populist call to arms against what he describes as Washington's unsustainable spending, crippling debt, career politicians, a 'socialist' health-care law and a failure to close the nation's borders to illegal immigrants."

"We've come to take our government back," Paul said during his victory speech. "The American people are not happy with what's going on in Washington. Tonight there is a tea party tidal wave, and we're sending a message to them. It's a message that I will carry with me on day one. It's a message of fiscal sanity, a message of limited government and balanced budgets."[16]

Senator-elect Rand Paul was absolutely right about one thing—there was a tea party tidal wave. The day after the election, the *New York Times* reported that the Tea Party had won five Senate and 39 House races with nine yet to be decided. Rand Paul would be joined in the Senate by fellow Tea Partiers Marco Rubio (R-FL), Mike Lee (R-UT), Pat Toomey (R-PA) and Ron Johnson (R-WI).[17]

Senate Democrats retained their majority by four seats but they would need six Republicans instead of just one to obtain cloture. So for all practical purposes, Minority Leader Mitch McConnell (R-KY) held a veto over all legislation and nominations considered by the full Senate.

That Tea Party wave did even more damage. Democrats lost a net 63 seats in the House of Representatives and, consequently, the speakership, their committee and subcommittee chairs and control of the all-important Rules Committee. Republicans would have 24 votes more than the 218 that decided all questions in the Committee of the Whole House. Those two dozen extra votes would enable them to freeze and frustrate the Obama agenda for the next two years.

The Republicans with help from their Tea Party allies picked up 12 governors: Rick Scott (R-FL), Terry Brandstad (R-IA), Sam Brownback (R-KS), Paul LePage (R-ME), Rick Snyder (R-MI), Susana Martinez (R-NM), John Kasich (R-OH), Mary Fallin (R-OK), Tom Corbett (R-PA), Bill Haslam (R-TN), Scott Walker (R-WI) and Matt Mead (R-WY). By contrast, the Democrats added Jerry Brown (D-CA), Dan Malloy (D-CT), Neil Abercrombie (D-HA) and Mark Dayton (D-MN). The warning posted on *Huffington Post* 10 months earlier went unheeded. Incumbent Democratic governors took a ferocious beating in 2010.

With congressional- and state-level redistricting set to occur after the 2010 census, the GOP swept states where they could lock in their gains for a decade or longer. The 23 GOP governors elected or reelected in 2010 (plus six more that were not up until 2011 or 2012) would lobby for and sign the legislation that tilted the control of their own legislatures and the Congress toward the Republican Party. And their map-makers would have lots of help, for Democrats also lost 27 legislative chambers and 680 state senators and state representatives.

All told, Democrats lost more than 750 incumbents due largely to their feckless efforts to address the jobs crisis. Those losses were their own fault. They made a conscious choice to nationalize the midterm elections and, essentially, make 2010 a referendum on President Obama and Obamacare. It was pure hubris, and that hubris would continue to dog the Democratic Party for three more election cycles.

Election night analysts, using the exit poll sponsored by their networks, reported that four out of five voters listed jobs and the economy as their most important issue. They also reported that 86 percent of voters said they were worried about the economy. And the shrewdest of those analysts drew the connection between the devastating losses suffered by the Democrats and their focus on health care when voters cared so deeply about jobs and were so worried about the economy.

On election night, however, no one talked about the role played by unemployed households in the results. Nor could they. Not all of the national exit poll's cross-tabs—the hundreds of pages of data that show how each question is answered by subgroups of survey respondents—were immediately available. Equally important, the cross-tabs for the state-level exit polls would not be available for public inspection for three to five weeks.

But buried under reams of computer printouts were some startling facts. Three in ten voters answered yes to the question "Has anyone in your household lost a job in the last two years." That 30 percent—more than three times the *official* unemployment rate and a dozen points higher than the *real* unemployment rate UCubed used—was a national number.

In the Ohio governor's race between Ted Strickland and John Kasich, 36 percent of voters reported having an unemployed person living in their household! In the Pennsylvania senate race between Joe Sestak and Pat Toomey, the unemployed households made up 34 percent of turnout. Ditto for the California senate race between Barbara Boxer and Meg Whitman. And, while the Democratic candidates won those unemployed households, narrowly in Ohio but by an overwhelming margin in Pennsylvania and California, only Senator Barbara Boxer's campaign had targeted the jobless in her campaign ads. Boxer won. Strickland and Sestak lost.

That pattern was replicated in every state with exit poll data. There were far more voters from unemployed households than anyone predicted.

They split their votes unevenly but tended to favor the Democratic candidate. And yet, only those Democrats who appealed directly to the jobless won.

Losing Democrats ignored the elephant in the room. For in each of those jobless households, at least one person had lost their job, their income stream and their self-esteem. Everyone else in that room knew what that meant, intimately. They also knew that it was not their father or mother's, brother or sister's fault. Their entire extended family was caught up in a grave national crisis that their political leaders never wanted to talk about.

The elephant in the room wasn't the guy or the gal who had lost their job. It was the mascot of the Republican Party that had stomped on that guy's hopes and blocked the changes that the gal had been promised. And by ignoring the jobs crisis completely and refusing to campaign for the votes from those jobless households in 2010, the Democratic leadership deserved the shellacking they received.

CHAPTER 18

HUMOR WORKS

My self-esteem has taken a major hit. I'm depressed and don't see any way out. I wish the good Lord would take me home at least I'd be with my husband then. I want to just give up, what good am I to any one like this...

Synthia's Unemployment Story

As the impact of the elections sunk in, tensions began rising within the Union of Unemployed. On its Facebook page, 3,000 jobs activists had become fans and 600 of them were commenting on our updates each week. Their comments ranged from cool-headed analysis to white-hot trash talk. Some sought clarity. Some asked for help. And some *liked* the updates and *shared* them with their friends and family members.

In late November, one post turned into a circular firing squad. The unemployed began taking pot shots at the 99ers, a term used to describe those who had exhausted their 99 weeks of unemployment benefits. And the 99ers fired back. In the hope of promoting comity, the ugliest of the *ad hominem* attacks were taken down from our page.

Several weeks later two of our strongest advocates, both women, started railing against Democratic Senator Debby Stabenow (MI), the sponsor of the "Americans Want to Work Act."[18] Stabenow's bill created a Tier 5—an additional 20 weeks of unemployment benefits for those living in states with 7.5 percent or higher unemployment rates. The Tier 5 was one of the 99ers' key demands and the issue that had sparked the earlier internecine fight.

Name-calling is an all-too-natural response when people are at their wits' end. These two women were well beyond that point. They had fought valiantly for the jobless, rallying others, e-mailing members of Congress and blogging about being unemployed. Something uniquely American—a belief that we can make things better and have the freedom to seek redress of grievances—died when they called it quits.

But you cannot blog without electricity, you cannot lobby when your heart is breaking and you cannot rally others if you've lost all hope. In a phone call to one of the women, I learned that she had been unemployed for so long that her savings were gone, her rent was long overdue and the electric company was threatening to shut off power. Like so many others, she was facing a powerful economic undertow all alone. And she knew she was drowning.[19]

Long, long ago, President Franklin Roosevelt had reminded Americans that "necessitous men are not free men. Liberty requires opportunity to make a living—living decent according to the standards of the time, a living which gives man not only enough to live by, but something to live for." But somehow too many members of Congress had forgotten his words.

On November 29, 2010, Senator Stabenow (D-MI) asked that her Tier 5 bill be adopted by unanimous consent. Senator George LeMieux (R-FL) objected and her bill died. LeMieux, an appointed but never elected senator, did not object to the $857-billion package extending the Bush-era tax cuts for the wealthiest Americans when it was rushed through the Senate a few weeks later.

Senator Bernie Sanders (D-VT), however, did conduct an eight-hour filibuster against the Bush tax extension deal hammered out between Vice President Joe Biden and Senate Minority Leader Mitch McConnell. Sanders, as he would in his 2016 presidential campaign, railed against the wealthiest Americans receiving multimillion dollar tax breaks. But even the lifelong socialist stopped short of refusing to give unanimous consent, as Senator Lemieux had, when faced with an $857-billion tax package.

His reasoning for not blocking the measure was motivated by a desire to give the working class any break they could get. Inside the Biden–McConnell deal there were provisions that meant working class Americans would not have to pay, on average, $2,000 more in taxes in 2012. Working Americans also would see no change in the 2 percent reduction in their payroll taxes, a provision of the American Recovery Act. There were provisions even the Union of Unemployed would support, including an investment tax credit for new equipment and a 13-month extension of unemployment benefits, both part of the 21-point *Hire US, America* plan.

A Tier 5 benefit was not included. Nor was the 65 percent COBRA discount.

The extension of the Bush tax cuts signaled a political sea change in the Congress—austerity measures driven by those lost tax revenues and the idling of so many wage earners became the Republican leadership's highest priority. As a result, they would derail every effort to put the unemployed, underemployed and uncounted back to work full-time. And that tension between austerity and prosperity would dominate the next decade.

But those fights lay over the horizon.

As UCubed celebrated its first birthday, we measured our growth and prepared for an uncertain future. The Union of Unemployed had grown to 2,360 members, 750 cubes and 35 neighborhoods (where three or more cubes were linked together). Its website saw 2 million visitors in 2010. Its broadcast e-mails reached 2.1 million inboxes. Via its pick-a-fight links, job activists delivered 60,000 emails to the White House and the Congress. And its cable television and online ads reached audiences numbering in the millions. Or, as a *New York Times* reporter noted, UCubed was fighting above its weight class.

The most intriguing development, however, was our on-going experiment with Facebook. Joyce Sheppard, a Machinists Communications Representative, started each day with a good morning post. Six to ten UCubed fans invariably responded with their own good wishes, which meant that their friends saw the original post. Facebook was a force-multiplier, as the military might say.

A simple change drove our Facebook reach sky high. Ms Sheppard added a photo of a cup of coffee with a smiley face drawn in its froth to her good morning post. And 60 fans liked or shared that posts. In no time, UCubed was saying good morning to an estimated 20,000 Facebook users each week. So serving up a new meme—a photo of a coffee cup and a caption—became a daily routine for the next five years.

Silly but effective at breaking down the isolation the jobless felt, the *coffee cup* meme experience led to other innovations. Some of our best Facebook innovations came through trial and error. The error was often mine. The trial—putting up with me—was Joyce Shepard's. And Saint Patrick's Day 2011 underscored our very different approaches.

In a long *Huffington Post* piece posted on March 17, I compared the British government's indifference to the Irish Famine of 1846–50 with our own government's indifference to the jobless. It quoted A. M. Sullivan, a young Ireland activist, reporting on conditions in the countryside:

> "The doomed people realized but too well what was before them. Last year's suffering exhausted them; a sort of stupor fell upon the people, contrasting remarkably with the fierce energy put forth a year before. It was no uncommon sight to see the cotter and his little family seated on the garden fence, gazing all day long in moody silence at the blighted plot that had been their last hope."[20]

Sullivan was later quoted as saying, "It would be utter injustice to deny that the government made exertions which, judged by ordinary circumstances, would be prompt and considerable. But judged by the awful magnitude of the evil then at hand or actually befallen, they were fatally tardy and inadequate."

Sullivan's evenhanded judgment could be applied to the Congress and the Obama administration. The original stimulus package was "prompt and considerable." Yet, their lack of focus on the "awful magnitude" of the Great Recession means any initiatives this year, or next, will be "fatally tardy and inadequate."

For millions of 99ers this "is a time of blight," I concluded. "Their careers, credit, savings and homes are forfeit. Hunger and homelessness, helplessness and hopelessness—those are the four horsemen of today's jobless."

Between the *Huffington Post* readership and the broadcast e-mail blast by UCubed, maybe, 30,000 people saw my overwrought essay. Joyce Sheppard, not surprisingly, had an antidote. She posted a photograph of a little dog dressed in a green vest and bowler with the words "top of the morning" splashed across it. In the next sixteen hours, it reached over a million Facebook users in the United States and around the globe.

Lesson learned. Humor works.

UCubed grew to 7,500 Facebook fans in March. A month later, it had 11,000 fans. Although it experienced a 20 percent increase in the number of job activists—those creating cubes on our website in 2011—the writing was on the wall. Facebook was enabling us to reach three-quarters of a million fans and their friends and family members each month; the website was seeing 30,000 visitors per month. A paradigm shift was making the UCubed website almost obsolete.

The cubing process that I hoped would allow us to grow exponentially could not come close to the reach of an engaged assortment of Facebook fans. So we began to think about a dramatic shift in strategy. Apparently, so were others.

In late May, both Paul Krugman, the Nobel Prize winning columnist for the *New York Times*, and former Labor Secretary Robert Reich endorsed the idea of a Works Progress Administration (WPA) style. UCubed had demanded such a jobs program since its launch in 2010; Tom Buffenbarger had argued for one in his *Chicago Tribune* op-ed in February 2009. Having Krugman and Reich weigh in changed the dynamic.

Such a WPA-style jobs initiative was the quickest way to put millions of Americans back to work. During 1935, the WPA had put today's equivalent of eight million people to work doing useful jobs with a lasting impact on this nation. And those WPA projects could be found in every state in the union.

Krugman, in his column "Against Learned Helplessness," reminded President Obama that "inventing reasons not to put the unemployed back to work is neither wise nor responsible. It is, instead, a grotesque abdication of responsibility."[21]

But Krugman, E. J. Dionne, Leo Hindery, Jr. and Bob Herbert were the only columnists who consistently advocated for the unemployed. Herbert, who had written his last column for the *New York Times* on March 19, was the best friend America's jobless ever had. He was fearless and forceful in denouncing the complete disconnect between the White House, the Congress and the jobs crisis. Dozens of other columnists and talking heads had gone silent. Or, worse still, cheered the last couple months of job growth and forgot about the 28.3 million Americans who remained unemployed, underemployed and uncounted.

And, if the Republicans in Congress led by Budget Committee Chairman Paul Ryan had their way, the jobless would be not just forgotten but buried forever under an avalanche of austerity measures. By mid-July 2011, the House Appropriations Committee was acting on Ryan's plan to cut $90 billion from the 2012 fiscal year budget. That was on top of the $38.5 billion slashed from the last half year of the fiscal year 2011. Both sets of cuts, severe austerity measures in their own right, were part of Ryan's 10-year plan to reduce federal spending by $6.6 trillion!

Given that the presidential primaries were less than six months away and Republican strategists on and off Capitol Hill saw Barack Obama as a one-term president, their strategy was clear. Use every opportunity to embarrass the president and deny him any legislative victories. The White House strategy was equally clear. Defend Obama's accomplishments, particularly Obamacare and the American Recovery and Reinvestment Act, and tout every decrease in the unemployment rate.

That clash of strategies would dominate the next six months. *Real* unemployment rate, however, stubbornly failed to do its part. While the *official* unemployment rate kept dropping, mostly because more and more people were leaving the workforce, the *real* unemployment rate held steady. According to Leo Hindery's analysis, it gyrated between 16.4 percent and 15.2 percent all year long. It began dipping ever so slightly in the last three months of 2011.

Meanwhile, elite Democratic opinion-makers ignored the obvious: by year's end, 27.4 million Americans were still looking for full-time jobs that paid well. Instead, they devised political strategies that would, eventually, doom not just the jobless but their party's reputation as a champion of the little guy.

CHAPTER 19

WHERE'S MY JOB, MR. PRESIDENT?

My wife is concerned that my depression is getting worse, although I do not know why it would. They tell us that unemployment is dropping. Could this be because so many like me are no longer on the unemployment roll because we have been forgotten about or overlooked?

Paul's Unemployment Story

A *New Republic* article caught my eye early July 2011. "The White Working Class: The Group That Will Likely Decide Obama's Fate" was written by Ray Teixeira. In it he argued that Obama needed only to match John Kerry's dismal showing among working class whites in 2004 to win reelection.

To Teixeira, the difference between victory and defeat in 2012 was a mere 5 percentage points. Obama lost working class whites in 2008 by 18 points. Kerry lost them by 23 points in 2004. So Obama could, theoretically, write off the demographic, lose it by Kerry's margin and still "survive pretty easily."

By switching from percentages to raw votes, Teixeira's point became clearer. Working class whites comprised 39 percent of all voters in 2008 or roughly 51 million raw votes. So, a shift of less than two million white working class voters would recreate Kerry's 2004 performance.

But 2012 wasn't going to be anything like 2008 or 2004. In the eight battleground states mentioned in Teixeira's "The White Working Class . . .," the *official* unemployment rate averaged 5.5 percent during John Kerry's campaign. In June 2011, the *official* rate in those states averaged 8.9 percent. The *real* unemployment rate was twice that last figure.

One of the assumptions underlying Teixeria's article was that African Americans, Hispanics, Asians and Millennials would be surge voters in 2012, just as they had been in 2008. Four years of population growth and their deepening allegiance to Obama would alleviate the need for Democrats to worry about white working class voters. There was, however, a fallacy built into his assumption.

The surge voters of 2008 were hammered by the Great Recession. In June 2011, the *official* unemployment rate was 16.2 percent for African Americans, 11.9 percent for Hispanics, 7.0 percent for Asians and 24.2 percent for Millennials. Their *real* unemployment rate was, again, twice as high.

By either set of statistics, 44 months after the Great Recession began—and a year after the White House's *summer of recovery*—minority communities still were experiencing unconscionably high levels of unemployment. Such persistent joblessness could turn into structural unemployment that, as the US census studies discussed earlier had shown, could lead to lower voter registration and turnout rates among the now structurally unemployed.

With even slightly lower turnout among what Teixeira would soon describe as the "rising American electorate," working class whites would become higher priority targets, presumably, for both political parties. Within days of Teixeira's *New Republic* article hitting the magazine stands, the presidential campaign of former Massachusetts Governor Mitt

Romney, the leading contender for the Republican nomination, was running a cable TV ad that reinforced what was at stake.

Romney, never much of a working class hero, started attacking President Obama for saying "there will always be bumps on the road to recovery" after the *official* unemployment rate hit 9.1 percent in May 2011. Romney's ad had actors rising up from a dusty roadbed to say, "I am an American, not a bump in the road." The ad showed a kaleidoscope of working class faces—white, black, brown, male, female, young and old. And, while the ad quickly disappeared, it had pinpointed a growing vulnerability for Barack Obama.

By September 2011, the *official* unemployment rate remained stuck at 9.1 percent. The all-in number, known as U-6, stood at 17.1 percent. Hindery's *real* unemployment number totaled 25.6 million Americans: 13.9 million unemployed added to 9.2 million involuntary part-time workers plus another 2.5 million discouraged workers. In its report for the month, the BLS noted that 43 percent of the unemployed had been out of work for at least 27 weeks!

Among Obama surge voters, those unconscionably high unemployment levels showed no signs of diminishing without direct intervention by the federal government. So, in an address to a joint session of Congress on September 8, 2011, President Obama argued for his version of a second stimulus bill. The body language of Republican members of Congress, particularly the facial expressions of House Speaker John Boehner, said it all. The American Jobs Act was dead on arrival.

In spite of its $447-billion price tag, the Obama proposals were pretty pedestrian. Three-fifths, or $253 billion, of its stimulus money came from payroll tax cuts, tax credits or tax relief for businesses. Meant to increase consumer demand in an election year, they did not affect, directly or immediately, the unemployed. If you weren't working, you weren't paying payroll taxes.

The cost of protecting teachers still in the classroom and modernizing schools—two key elements of Obama's American Jobs Act—tallied $65 billion. But again, that money did not affect, directly and immediately, the unemployed. Some unemployed teachers might be rehired, some construction workers might find temporary work, but the numbers that might be helped did not match the millions of Americans who desperately needed to get back to work.

Surface transportation, an infrastructure bank, a veterans' initiative and the rehab of vacant property—all excellent ideas—reflected the mistaken impression that America's jobless were mainly blue collar workers. Many were, but tens of millions had worn white collars or had worked in a shrinking retail sales workforce. So the $75 billion allocated for those excellent ideas did not affect, directly or immediately, the overwhelming majority of the unemployed.

That left $54 billion, or 12 percent of the proposed spending, for the extension of unemployment benefits, unemployment insurance reforms and what the White House called a "Pathways Back to Work Fund." And yes, those three programs did affect, directly and immediately, the unemployed. So did the bill's provision to prohibit employers from discriminating against the unemployed when hiring. One of the *Hire Us, America* proposals, the anti-discrimination section, was the only provision that had universal and urgent application.

The America Jobs Act proposed by the president did not contain a modern-day version of the CCC or the WPA. But it did raise taxes and, consequently, it ran counter to the Republican Party's long standing policy on cutting taxes. The bill's spending proposals also ran counter to the GOP's long-planned austerity measures. Furthermore, no Republican was about to hand Barack Obama a legislative victory on the eve of a presidential campaign.

So, while the Union of Unemployed urged its 25,000 jobs activist to weigh in on the American Jobs Act and urge its adoption with amendments that added those CCC and WPA programs, I knew that the president's speech and his subsequent campaign stops hammering Republicans for not passing his bill were pure political theatre. The bill was designed to be dead on arrival. No hearings were ever held, no votes were ever taken and no jobs were ever created.

The American Jobs Act was, at best, a political ruse. At worst, it was a cruel, cynical ploy by a Democratic president. For the real battle, a battle being waged behind closed doors even as the president campaigned for his bill, was over $1.5 trillion in spending cuts, not $447 billion in tax cuts and spending increases.

And $1.5 trillion in spending cuts tend to concentrate minds on Capitol Hill, for everyone's sacred cows were about to be gored. And the unemployed? Well, they don't vote so they don't count.

On October 14, five weeks after Obama's speech, congressional committees reported their proposals for slashing billions from the programs under their jurisdiction. The Joint Committee on Deficit Reduction, with its six senators and six members of Congress equally divided between Republicans and Democrats, then began cobbling together $1.5 trillion in spending cuts or tax increases in order to meet their Thanksgiving deadline. The Senate and the House then had to approve those $1.5 trillion in draconian cuts—half in defense and half in domestic spending—by Christmas. If they did not, those cuts occurred automatically on New Year's Day.

Ten days later, on October 24, President Obama admitted the obvious. His American Jobs Act was going nowhere:

> "Without a doubt, the most urgent challenge that we face right now is getting our economy to grow faster and to create more jobs . . . we can't wait for an increasingly dysfunctional Congress to do its job. Where they won't act, I will."

His bravado was impressive. But a series of executive orders could never help 28.3 million Americans get back to work. Nor could the series of deep cuts in food stamps, Medicaid and unemployment benefits that the Deficit Reduction Committee was kicking around behind those closed doors. Only a modern day version of the WPA could put so many back to work.

So, the Union of Unemployed launched an iconic Facebook campaign that asked, "Where's MY Job, Mr. President?" It starred sepia photographs taken under the auspices of the WPA back in the 1930s. It also recounted the accomplishments of the WPA. Those factoids were meant to reinforce the idea that, if we did it once, we could do it again.

In a broadcast e-mail to UCubed leaders, activists and fans, I explained that the WPA employed 2.7 million Americans in 1935, 2.3 million in 1936, 1.7 million in 1937 and 2.9 million in 1938. Over 9.7 million jobless Americans received WPA paychecks over those four years. Owing to the growth in our nation's workforce, today's equivalent four-year tally would exceed 27.4 million, roughly a million less than our nation's real unemployment level in October 2011.

What had the WPA done? According to *American-Made*[22], a book by Nick Taylor, the WPA

built 650,000 miles of roads, 78,000 bridges, 125,000 civilian and military buildings, built, improved or enlarged 800 airports and 700 miles of airport runways;

served almost 900 million hot lunches to school children and operated 150,000 nursery schools;

presented 225,000 concerts to audiences totaling 150 million;

performed plays, vaudeville acts, puppet shows and circuses before 30 million people and

produced 475,000 works of art and at least 276 full-length books and 701 pamphlets.

Taylor emphasized that the statistics were "silent on the transformation of the infrastructure that occurred, the modernization of the country, the malnutrition defeated and the educational prospects gained, the new horizons opened."

For the next nine months, an ever-changing set of memes—photos and factoids about the WPA—would be posted to the UCubed Facebook page and, on a monthly basis, one new meme would act as the cover photo of its Facebook page. The tag line "Where's MY Job, Mr. President?" became the focal point for paid ads designed to recruit new Facebook fans for UCubed. Those ads slowly and very deliberately built up our activist base and expanded our reach until UCubed had the largest Facebook page in the American labor movement.

Eventually, word filtered back that the White House was not exactly pleased by our constant demands for jobs. The fact that the UCubed campaign was designed to remind Democratic leaders (and potential voters) of the party's traditions and values did not lessen the White House's discomfort level. Our blog posts and memes had hit a nerve, a nerve made overly sensitive by the president's declining approval ratings among the unemployed.

In late October 2011, the *New York Times* surveyed the unemployed. The newspaper had conducted a similar survey in December 2009. Taken together, those polls showed a not-so-subtle shift in the attitudes of jobless Americans.

President Obama got much higher marks than the Congress did. Only 10 percent of the unemployed approved of what the Congress had done. By comparison, Obama's overall approval rating was 40 percent but down 21 points from two years earlier. On handling the economy, the president had slipped from 57 percent to 32 percent approval. On job creation, he had fallen from 47 percent to 29 percent in two years.

Hidden in the cross-tabs of the two *New York Times* surveys were even more dramatic shifts. Americans' self-perceptions were changing in ways that would alter the political landscape for three election cycles or, perhaps, even longer. In 2009, 37 percent of the unemployed described themselves as middle class. Two years later, only 22 percent did so. In 2009, 17 percent of the jobless said they were lower class. By 2011, that number had grown to 27 percent.

Most importantly, 46 percent of those surveyed in 2011 answered working class, an increase of five points. In what was supposedly a classless society, nearly three-quarters of the jobless were comfortable calling themselves working class or lower class. That shift had huge implications for the tone-deaf politicians and their strategists whose campaigns had always appealed solely to middle-class voters.

For the 2012 presidential and congressional elections, the *New York Times* poll of the jobless meant that estimated 40 million voters would come from households where a mother or father, son or daughter, sister or brother had been unemployed in the last four years. Each one of those voters knew exactly what it meant to be unemployed, underemployed or uncounted. Each one knew exactly how far down the economic ladder he or she had fallen. And their fall from middle class to working or lower class was felt by every member of their immediate and extended family.

Those 40 million voters—one-third of the expected turnout in 2012— would not move in lockstep. But 40 million voters could split unevenly and boost one presidential candidate's chances over his opponent's. As Rex Teixeira pointed out, dismissively, a shift of a couple million white working class voters might not impact President Obama's chances.

But then, again, those 40 million voters from unemployed households were never part of Teixeira's new "coalition of the ascendant."

CHAPTER 20

COALITION OF THE ASCENDANT

When you have no income, you shop at the dollar store and even then you are counting your pennies. It's hard. It's scary. I just hope that our government wakes up and takes a good long look at the people who are struggling. They don't care, they have a job ... what about the little guy? What about those of us who want to work, who want to be a contributing member of society again ...

Lori's Unemployment Story

Each of the millions of broadcast e-mails sent out since UCubed launched two years earlier ended with "In Unity—Strength" followed by my signature. That complimentary close was more than a personal trademark. It was the philosophy behind the Union of Unemployed, specifically, and the philosophy of the labor movement, more generally, as it pursued universal solidarity.

And yet, as 2012 began, divisiveness was what mattered.

The Center for American Progress, an elite progressive think tank, issued "The Path to 270: Demographics versus Economics in the 2012 Elections." The 64-page document, co-written by Rex Teixeira and John

Halpin, argued that "President Obama should build a 'coalition of the ascendant' made up of minorities, Millennials, single women and college educated whites." If you weren't part of that "coalition of the ascendant," you were "rooted in the declining sector of whites," according to the paper's authors.

As outrageous as that proposition was, the fact that it was implicitly endorsed by the Center for American Progress, led by John Podesta and Neera Tanden, was an abomination. Both had been senior advisors to the 2008 Obama and Clinton campaigns, respectively, both had significant White House experience dating back to Bill Clinton's presidency and both were likely to play outsized roles in future presidential campaigns.

I was not the only one to be taken aback by their "The Path to 270..." Tom Edsall opened his *New York Times* blog post with this observation:

> "For decades, Democrats have suffered continuous and increasingly severe losses among white voters. But preparations by Democratic operatives for the 2012 election make it clear for the first time that *the party will explicitly abandon the white working class.*"

The emphasis is mine. But the strategy harmed all *small d* Democrats. In another broadcast e-mail, I explained why that was so.

Teixeira and Halpin argued that the white working class voted for John McCain over Barack Obama by a 17-point margin, then voted for the GOP by a 30-point margin in 2010 and, therefore, were irretrievably lost to Obama. They blithely overlooked the math behind those numbers.

With a 17-point margin, at least 41 percent of the white working class voted for Obama. Take those 41 points off the board and McCain wins in a walk. Even with a 30-point margin, 35 percent of white working class voters still supported Democratic congressional candidates. Shift those 35 points to the GOP and the Republicans would control not just the House of Representatives but the Senate as well.

Teixeira and Halpin argued that demographics trump economics. While conceding that high unemployment existed in the battleground states and that that made winning them more problematic, their strategy overlooked the fact that jobless households in those states contained Blacks, Latinos, Millennials, the college educated and single women—their so-called "coalition of the ascendant"—and white working class Democrats, too. The fact that 30 percent of all voters came from jobless households seem to have escaped them. So, too, did the fact that they were writing off 40 million Americans, half of whom had voted for congressional Democrats just two years earlier.

But elite opinion counts. It counts double if it receives the imprimatur of the Center for American Progress. So my counterargument took a more emotional tack:

> "Since when do Democrats discriminate on the basis of race, age, gender and education?
>
> When did the Democrats become the party of the fashionably and upwardly mobile? When did the party adopt a platform so openly dismissive of those forced on the down escalator of life by hard times or field candidates that turned their back on Americans mired in poverty . . . retired and living on social security . . . or married with children?
>
> When, exactly, did the Democrats abandon those who decide not to go to college, who work with their brains and brawn, who develop their skills as apprentices and then use them as journeymen, who wait tables, run drop presses, dig coal, weld pipes, stock groceries, paint bridges or empty bed pans?"

My temper tantrum ended with "apparently, I missed the media advisory announcing that the Democrats were striking their big tent and replacing it with an encampment of pup tents—one for each of the demographic groups chosen for the 'coalition of the ascendant.'"

What I said did not matter, nor did how I said it. The die was cast. The Obama presidential campaign adopted "The Path to 270 . . ." as its campaign's bible. The unemployed were relegated to the coalition of the downwardly mobile.

No clearer indication of which direction the Democratic party was taking could be found than in President Obama's State of the Union speeches. The words *jobless* or *unemployed* were never heard in his 2012 address to Congress, nor in his State of the Union speeches in 2010 or 2011. So, for three years running while the *real* unemployment number remained above 28 million, the president had nothing to say in his most important and most watched speech of the year to those Americans who were unemployed, underemployed or uncounted.

But *they* had lots to say in their own way about politicians in general. In early February, UCubed posted a meme on its Facebook page that said, "diapers and politicians should be changed often and for the same reason." More than 15,000 UCubed fans liked or shared that joke. It quickly reached 4.5 million of their friends and family members.

A couple months later, UCubed posted another meme using a Milton Berle quote, "You can send a man to Congress but you can't make him think." It was liked or shared 102,000 times in 24 hours. All their friends saw it—all 27 million of them.

For the jobless, laughter was a medicine they could afford. They were laughing, mostly, at incumbents—never a good sign if you're running for reelection—and they weren't doing so in a lighthearted way. They were getting damn tired of being ignored. Their anger was becoming omni-directional; any and every incumbent would feel their wrath, including the incumbent president.

A *Washington Post/ABC News* survey released in late May 2012 drove that point home. White jobless voters gave Mitt Romney a 24-point advantage over Barack Obama beating him by 58 percent to 34 percent!

Jobless voters, including African Americans, Latinos, Asians and whites, split 55 percent for Romney and 45 percent for Obama, a much narrower 10-point margin.

Two questions underscored the political crisis facing Democrats from the top of the ticket to the bottom. When asked if anyone living in their household had been laid off or lost their job, 35 percent of the respondents said yes. When asked if they knew close friends or immediate family members who had been laid off or lost their jobs in the last few years, *71 percent said they did.*

The coalition of the downwardly mobile was growing. The *Washington Post/ABC News* poll meant the number of jobless households had increased from 30 percent to 35 percent since 2010. And that meant voters with an intimate knowledge of the unemployed would cast more than 46 million votes in an election that was rapidly approaching.

And the "coalition of the ascendant"? Well, the horse race question in that *Washington Post/ABC News* survey showed Obama leading Romney by 49 percent to 45 percent. So there was no reason to throw away their campaign bible. "The Path to 270 . . ." folks remained convinced that the path to victory lay through that encampment of pup tents.

CHAPTER 21

HONEY AND BUZZ E BEE

... if I can't get a job in this market, where does that leave everyone else who worked hard all their entire lives, only to be shown the door? What angers me more is politicians playing games, trying to make the unemployed look like they are asking for handouts, what all most truly want is a decent job ... I'm 27 years old and I know that things will get better for me eventually. I only hope that as my generation grows older, we remember the hardships of those who came before us and ensure that hard-working, well-meaning people do not have to suffer like this ever, ever again.

Dana's Unemployment Story

By the time the *Washington Post/ABC News* poll was released, UCubed had more than 100,000 activists. It was reaching 1.3 million Facebook users each week. And, according to Facebook, UCubed fans had 27.4 million *friends of fans*—those were their friends and family members who they could share a post or meme with just by hitting the *like* or *share* button.

Because virtually all of our fans lived in those jobless households, UCubed had the potential of reaching roughly three-fifths of those 46 million voters. And we could do so for pennies on the dollar as compared to the traditional methods of voter contact. Later on, as Facebook changed its algorithms, it would become more costly to reach so many millions of users. But in those early days, Facebook was more interested in expansion than it was in advertising revenue.

Over the winter, Glenn Totten, who ran a successful communications company, and I had bounced around ideas for a multi-week, Facebook-centered campaign aimed at the broader target audience of *friends of fans*. Totten was an artist when it came to producing television ads, had spent decades producing campaign ads for Democratic candidates and had produced ads for UCubed since its launch. I hoped that somehow he could turn my crazy, off-the-wall ideas into an ad that actually resonated with voters.

This effort was different. Facebook had not yet developed a workable platform for videos. So, our posts and memes would have to point UCubed fans and their friends toward a landing page where they could click on the ads. And the ads had to use cartoon-like animations because, well, how else are you going to show bees stinging an elephant?

My original concept was to show a swarm of worker bees attacking a pachyderm. Believe it or not, there is scientific evidence that elephants are deathly afraid of bees. Scientists had put the theory into practice in order to protect African villages from herds of elephants by playing the sounds of a bee swarm over loudspeakers. The elephants took the hint and headed out into the grasslands.

Totten thought I was nuts. The link to the unemployed was tenuous at best. There were millions of worker bees but the unemployed were not working. So what was the connection? While the GOP mascot had been an elephant going back to the cartoons of Thomas Nast, how do you turn a lumbering grey behemoth into an evil, hive-crushing, jobs-destroying brute? The answer lay not in the animation but in the storyboards that carried the core message, "BEE MAD @ THE GOP."

Led by anthropomorphized characters "Buzz E Bee" and his wife "Honey Bee," the campaign would tell the story of the worker bees whose hives and lives were destroyed by the big, bad elephants. It would pin the worker bees' plight as a big red and white target on the butt of the Grand Old Party's mascot. And, in the closing weeks of the election, the worker bees would be urged to swarm to the polls and hand those big, bad elephants a stinging defeat.

As pitched to Tom Buffenbarger and the IAM executive council, the campaign was built around 12 micro-videos, each lasting less than 20 seconds. Starting in late July, the campaign continued until election day or roughly for 15 weeks. Accompanied by an aggressive Facebook advertising effort, it simultaneously attracted attention and increased the number of UCubed activists by 50,000 Facebook fans. Ultimately, we believed it would deliver 90 million message units to *friends of fans*.

The rationale for spending $150,000 or more on this wild idea was two-fold. First, the Machinists had spent three years building up UCubed so that the jobless could have a major impact on the 2012 election. Using our 100,000 (or eventually 150,000) Facebook activists to reach out to even half of their 30 or 35 million friends was one way to ensure that they did have an impact. Second, the unemployed did not differentiate between friends and foes, Democrats or Republicans. Their anger was omni-directional; they hated all incumbents. So channeling their anger at their real tormentors—BEE MAD @ THE GOP—offered the dual benefit of defeating our foes and helping our friends in a very volatile political environment.

Somehow Buffenbarger convinced his colleagues to go along with my fantastic (some might say hare-brained) scheme. Our creative team sprang into action. Totten went to work on scripts and storyboards. Ian Lurie and his team at Portent, a social media communications company, started building the landing page. Adele Pollis produced graphics. LaToya Egwuekwe and Joyce Shepard planned and produced packages of tweets, posts and memes to accompany the micro-videos. I wrote a couple dozen broadcast e-mails. When I explained our concept to other labor and political leaders, I only sought to keep them from laughing out loud at our approach.

But the laughter grew to a crescendo. Among the unemployed.

By October 3, our BEE MAD @ THE GOP campaign had reached 29.9 million Facebook users, created 147 million impressions, generated 1.2 million shared stories and 1.9 million created stories and produced, on average, a daily organic reach of 2.1 million. Our wacky micro-videos about Buzz E Bee, Honey Bee and the GOP PAC-y-derms were downloaded 1.3 million times. And it looked like we were on track to hit 2.5 million video downloads by election day.

Every single day, more than 33,000 UCubed fans engaged in the oldest political activity in the world: talking over the back fence with their friends and neighbors via one of the newest political tools, Facebook. On average, our total daily reach exceeded 890,000 Facebook users. Only the *Wall Street Journal*, *USA Today* and *The New York* times reached more folks on a daily basis than UCubed did.

And for the first time since the Great Recession started, jobless Americans were putting their own personal stamp of approval on a compelling . . . hyper-partisan . . . and persuasive message. BEE MAD @ THE GOP was moving numbers, huge numbers.

UCubed's successes through those first 10 weeks were communicated to labor leaders, Democratic congressional and senate campaign managers, indirectly to White House operatives and array of public policy advocates. The memo urged them to "meet and listen to jobless voters in your district or state. With two more unemployment reports to be released before November 6, the jobless and their families are focused on but one thing: How will your candidate or your opponent end their long financial and personal nightmare."

The BEE MAD campaign kept hammering on the Republicans citing their votes against the unemployed and their demeaning statements about the jobless. The facts, buttressed with a bit of humor, spoke for themselves:

> Ever since 2008 the Grand Old Party has been on a rampage. Like a herd of rogue elephants the GOP destroyed our homes and lives, wiped out our life savings and then ambled away—scot free—with billions in tax cuts, billions in bailouts and millions in bonuses. Jobless Americans have 8,000 reasons to BEE MAD @ THE GOP (followed by a list of the votes cast against the unemployed).

> GOP leaders weren't stupid. They used unemployment extensions as the rock on which to leverage what they really wanted—lower taxes for the wealthy, deeper spending cuts and fewer regulations on business. Last year, during the debt committee fiasco and the consolidated appropriations bill of 2011 (both must pass pieces of legislation), the GOP held the jobless hostage each time. "Give us tax breaks and spending cuts," they said, "or else we won't extend unemployment benefits."

> GOP leaders called us "hobos" ... said we were "spoiled" ... claimed that if we received unemployment, we'd just "blow it on drugs" ... thought we needed "tough love" ... felt we should be housed in state penitentiaries and forced to take lessons in "personal hygiene" ... and worse. How much worse? The GOP Lieutenant Governor of South Carolina said that he was told "as a small child to quit feeding the animals. You know why? Because they breed. You're facilitating the problem if you give an animal or person ample food supply. They will reproduce, especially the ones that don't think too much farther than that."

> The GOP attack on worker bees never lets up. More hives and lives will be destroyed. More honey will be stolen. And until they're handed a stinging defeat, the GOP will remain relentless. But did you know that

bees can stampede elephants? So let's go ahead and make their lives as miserable as they've made ours. Stampede the elephants. Join the swarm.

Why are elephants afraid of bees? Bees are smart. Bees communicate. And when riled, worker bees swarm to the defense of their hives. As elephants have learned—and elephants never forget—that their tough hide isn't where bees sting. They swarm inside their trunk, around their eyes and mouths and under their tails. Bee venom is excruciatingly painful, even toxic.

Protecting one's honey comes naturally to worker bees. But what if the intruders pillaged their hives, stomped on the worker bees and squeezed every ounce of honey from their combs. Would you still attack, if you knew it was the last thing you would ever do? If you were a worker bee, you would. No matter how massive the intruders are, worker bees attack their tormentors, swarming by the thousands, stinging the most sensitive tissue.

Each of those storyboard outlines were turned into animated cartoons by Glenn Totten and the folks at Totten Communications. They would win the first Pollie awarded by the American Society of Political Consultants for the best use of Facebook in "Get Out the Vote" campaign for their work on BEE MAD @ THE GOP.

As zany, crazy or unhinged as you might think the campaign was, Speaker John Boehner's Super PAC paid it the highest compliment. It ran a bee-and-honey-comb-based television ad in an Ohio congressional campaign. The UCubed bees, Buzz E and Honey, were getting noticed. And they were moving numbers.

During the campaign, 4 million videos were downloaded on Facebook. But the UCubed engagement level went far deeper. Every day it had 33,000 engaged users, an army of the unemployed who did not go door to door but with a click of their mouse shared messages with, on average,

275 of their friends and family members. That level of engagement with *friends of fans* increased our *total daily reach* to 858,000 Facebook users.

Over the course of our 101-day campaign, the UCubed total daily reach added up to 82.4 million message units, about 10 percent fewer than we had originally projected. That 82 million number, even to me, seemed beyond believable. But those were that statistics that Facebook produced and we had no way to independently verify them. All we knew was that UCubed was experimenting with an incredibly powerful new political tool that would change politics forever.

And we knew one more thing.

Back in spring, the *Washington Post/ABC News* survey had Mitt Romney beating Barack Obama among the unemployed by 10 points, 55 percent to 45 percent. The exit polls on November 6, 2012, had Obama beating Romney among the unemployed by 10 points, 55 percent to 45 percent. That twenty-point swing could not be attributable to UCubed alone. The Obama–Biden campaign did stellar work. Romney's crack about "the 47 percent who were the 'takers'" certainly helped.

But UCubed and its BEE MAD @ THE GOP campaign deserved more credit than it ever received. It had convinced its target audience to act, to hit that *like* or *share* button on Facebook and, in so doing, to make a very personal yet very political endorsement that they knew their friends and family members would see. That they delivered more than 82 million messages in that way was a historic achievement. That the UCubed campaign empowered so many jobless Americans to fight back against their tormentors was unprecedented. But that those without jobs, without hope and without much encouragement, if any, continued to support a Democratic leadership that had abandoned them was simply incredible.

Against all odds, those jobless activists changed American politics forever. Others would copy what they did, others would pour money into building a Facebook infrastructure, others would test how best to engage their own activists and still others would use Facebook as force-multiplier.

Not surprisingly, those *others* would *not* be the *big D* Democrats nor the labor unions representing worker bees. Instead, the PAC-y-derms took their stinging defeat to heart and decided to invest heavily in social media.

CHAPTER 22

BREAKOUT YEAR

I've been unemployed for four years. Lost my job because the company I worked for said they were downsizing. Found my job posted on Monster the next day with a Bachelors Degree added to it. I was "pissed." But there was nothing I could do about it ... I've been sad, mad, depressed, going thru a divorce now. My life fell apart.

Jan's Unemployment Story

President Obama won his second term by 4 million votes. As impressive as that sounds, his 2008 margin of victory had been cut in half, down from 7.9 million votes. And that decrease was due, in large measure, to the ongoing ravages of the Great Recession.

In the second quarter of 2012, the broadest measure of unemployment—U-6—had reached depression levels in most battleground states. Their unemployed, underemployed and discouraged workers—Nevada (16.9 percent), Michigan (14.7 percent), Florida (13.9 percent), North Carolina (13 percent), Pennsylvania (12.5 percent), Ohio (12.5 percent), Wisconsin (11.4 percent) and Minnesota (10 percent)—still carried the scar tissue a little more than a year later. And those eight states were responsible for shedding 1.8 million votes from Obama's 2008 margin.

Not surprisingly, six big red states sliced another 1.1 million off Obama's 2008 margin. And they, too, experienced depression-level unemployment. In Kentucky (14 percent), Tennessee (13.6 percent), West Virginia (12.7 percent), Indiana (12 percent) and Texas (10.7 percent), U-6 captured both the broader unemployment rate and, consequently, the deepening angst of their citizens who were voting their empty wallets.

So, all told, 2.9 million of the 3.9 million votes that Obama lost came from just 13 states, all of which had double-digit unemployment levels not so long ago. Cause and effect? Maybe. Maybe not. But economics often trumps demographics in presidential politics. And some of those same double-digit employment states would still be in double digits in 2016 and would provide the Republicans a decisive margin of victory in the Electoral College.

No one was prescient enough to see the distant future that clearly. Their crystal balls—and mine—were filled with the blinding blizzards so many holiday ornaments contain. It was impossible to see the figurines until their snowflakes settled. In presidential politics, that took longer than one might imagine.

For the Union of Unemployed, 2013 was a year of transition. With encouragement from the Machinists, UCubed reinvented itself as a miniature Super PAC, one able to lobby more aggressively if we so chose, one able to continue to communicate with the unemployed via Facebook and one more capable of being directly involved in political campaigns and endorsing candidates. The reinvention meant creating a new nonprofit organization, securing sustainable financing, continuing to advocate for the unemployed and trying to educate Democratic candidates about the inherent power of that key voting bloc. It would not be easy.

In a pre-election memo to Tom Buffenbarger and the IAM executive council, I explained that "the fights ahead are few and far between. In 2013, Virginia and New Jersey have gubernatorial races that pit incumbents with high approval ratings against, at this time, total unknowns. It is not until 2014 when the gubernatorial, senatorial and congressional campaigns heat up that UCubed could have an impact, politically." The memo explained that

> "The powers-that-be, including both Democrats and Republicans, are hell bent on austerity. And that means even deep cuts in programs that serve core Democratic constituencies—Blacks, Latinos, seniors, the jobless, government employees and blue collar workers of all hues.

> And while the lame duck Congress will either deal with or punt on sequestration (the 1.5 trillion dollars in spending cuts discussed in Chapter 19), extending the Bush tax cuts and Obama's payroll tax cut, the fact is that most of 2013 will be taken up with a series of legislative battles over the GOP's promises to cut the federal deficit, not raise the debt ceiling, 'reform' of Medicaid, Medicare and Social Security and push through steep cuts in appropriations. Those battles will be replicated on the state level by GOP-led legislatures.

> The attached Facebook lander—Exit Left Ahead—captures the overarching strategy for the campaigns UCubed must fight in the months ahead. Keep banging away at the heartless austerity plans and keep pushing a small 'd' democratic alternative that leads to prosperity. And to do that UCubed will have to focus more on policy than politics."

The memo ended with a request for an annual commitment of a quarter million dollars, half to pay salaries and expenses and half to engage in a Facebook-centric advertising program designed to grow the number of its fans and engage *friends of fans* in the legislative battles ahead.

As would become a standard practice for the next three years, Buffenbarger sought and received the requisite commitments from his colleagues. UCubed, once a community service project of the Machinists, would still be financed (mostly) by the IAM's generosity and a staff person would serve on its new board of directors. But it was incumbent upon UCubed to find and cultivate other sources of revenue.

Throughout the year, the "Exit Left Ahead" campaign used a green interstate highway sign to suggest the path forward. Symbolically the towns of prosperity and austerity were the choices drivers faced as the highway split left and right. That landing page added more than 60,000 new fans of UCubed during its relatively brief lifespan.

But we had lots help from an unexpected source in 2013: Republicans.

One of the challenges UCubed always faced was engaging its fans in non-election years. The jobless who were drawn to our Facebook page were not traditional activists who cared so deeply about an issue that they wanted to grab a pitchfork and go poke a congressperson. Most still hoped to be called back to work or start a new job. Instinctively they knew that they would not advance their careers by carrying signs, attending demonstrations or marching in Washington. They also knew that discrimination against the unemployed existed and that human resources departments would check social media for politically offensive posts.

What they knew and politicians did not was that when the Great Recession began, corporate America targeted employees in the prime of their careers. Those born between 1947 and 1953, the core of the baby boom generation, were in positions of real responsibility—senior vice presidents, middle managers, foremen and women, executive secretaries, sales representatives, accountants, agents brokers and producers—and many were drawing six-figure salaries.

Most had college degrees, three decades of experience in their chosen fields, homes in communities where their children attended the local high school before heading off to college and voting histories dating back to 1972. They were, in short, solid citizens who were being prematurely retired.

Their former employers proved to be equal opportunity firers. Men and women felt the axe in equal numbers. But by 2011, those searching for work included 2.4 million from management or professional ranks, 2.7 million from service occupations and 3.1 million from sales and office careers. By 2013, nearly 2 million men and women over the age of 55 were *officially* unemployed and another 1.9 million were underemployed or discouraged workers.

Older, wizened and far more cynical, the prematurely retired were one of the most potent forces in American politics. They were registered voters with a chip on their shoulders—their careers had been cut short for reasons completely out their control. So they were intensely interested in what Washington was doing. They were shrewd enough to know that a Congress led by Mitch McConnell, John Boehner and Eric Cantor would not necessarily have their best interests in mind. And they certainly would not mind sharing a joke or two at their tormentors' expense.

That by-now infamous U-6 was stuck above 15 percent nationwide and 42 states were above its 10 percent unemployment level. Its sister statistics U-1, U-2, U-3, U-4 and U-5 ranged 3.8 percent to 8.5 percent unemployed.

Seeing that line up, however, reminded me how German submarines were numbered in World War II. They, too, had been numbered consecutively from U-1 to U-4717. Called U-boats, they fought without restraint, attacked without warning and seldom rescued survivors. Their captains and crews proved to be remorseless killing machines often operating in packs to maximize the carnage.

In a leap to gallows humor, the current U-6 of 14 percent became a metaphor for an equally remorseless machine stalking and torpedoing our economy. And the officers manning the bridge of that specific U-boat were none other than the senate minority leader, speaker of the House and the House majority whip. I called it McConnell's Navy and had Glenn

Totten turn Mitch McConnell, John Boehner and Eric Cantor into cartoon characters.

And boy, were they easy targets. The cartoon version of McConnell played the martinet, Boehner played the slightly sauced second-in-command and Cantor came across as the kiss-ass backstabber. Unfortunately, as much fun as posting these cartoons were, the GOP Congress was convinced that its efforts to torpedo Obamacare were no laughing matter. They were prepared to shut down the government to make their point.

By Labor Day 2013, UCubed had grown to 151,000 fans. Theoretically, they had 43.1 million friends of fans because each of our fans had, according to Facebook, an average of 285 friends. And that growth spurt came just in the nick of time.

On October 5, the *New York Times* reported that "shortly after President Obama started his second term, a loose-knit coalition of conservative activists led by former Attorney General Edwin Meese III gather in the capitol to plot strategy."

They produced a "little-notice blueprint to defunding Obamacare . . . that articulated a take-no-prisoners legislative strategy . . . that could derail the health care overhaul if conservative leaders were willing to push Republicans—including their cautious leaders—into cutting off financing for the entire federal government."

That blueprint was endorsed by 46 of the biggest names in the Tea Party wing of the Republican Party. It seemed that for the last eight months, they had worked under the radar screens to turn that blueprint into reality. Then they shut down government offices, filled the airwaves with incendiary rhetoric, encircled the nation's capital with truck convoys, stacked barricades around the White House and demanded that a crisis of their own making end but only on their terms.

It was a coup d'état. And "McConnell's Navy" was smack dab in the thick of it. So UCubed simply reposted an earlier cartoon showing the U-6 taking aim at the USS America, firing all its torpedoes and, much to its leaders' chagrin, seeing those torpedoes circle back to sink the U-6.

Glub, glub.[23]

UCubed, however, was on the rise. Since launching its "McConnell's Navy" campaign, it had added 22,000 fans and an estimated 8 million friends of fans. It had also launched a Spanish language Facebook page that grew to 4,000 fans. The cumulative audience for the animated videos exceeded 1.1 million. During the government shutdown, UCubed was reaching 1.4 million fans per week, a level not seen since the 2012 presidential campaign.

The momentum strategy created for UCubed—a steady growth in fans and a constant emphasis on engaging them in order to reach their friends of fans—worked. With now 163,000 fans, UCubed became the largest Facebook page in the American labor movement. Teamsters (135,000), AFL-CIO (110,000) and AFSCME (68,000) were its closest competitors.

Among organizations based in the United States, UCubed had broken into the top 50 and ranked above the World Wildlife Fund (#50) and behind Princeton (#44) and UCLA (#21). But in each instance our engagement level, weirdly called "People Talking About That" by Facebook, was two to three times that of the universities named.

The year 2013 was a breakout year for UCubed. For the unemployed and underemployed and uncounted? Not so much. The BLS reported that U-6, the unemployment stat, had dropped from 14.5 percent in January to 13.7 percent by October. Hindery's *real* unemployment rate stood a tad lower at 13.6 percent, which, with the other workers who wanted a job, meant that there were still 24.8 million Americans looking for full-time work with good pay and benefits 71 months after the Great Recession began.

CHAPTER 23

A SPEECHWRITER, NOT

I have been unemployed for over five years [not] because I lack motivation, or intelligence, or because I cannot pass a drug test, [but] because I won't "settle" for something less than my ideal job … Under normal circumstances, I am a very high achiever; a perfectionist, even. I can't, for the life of me, figure out why no one, no one at all, has give[n] me a chance.

M.E.'s Unemployment Story

One of the unique pleasures of presidential politics is the friendships forged in the midst of a contest. Not the acquaintances made nor the names added to contacts lists, but the real friendships that last for years if not decades are the joys that come with victory or defeat. Those friendships take on a life of their own, one that can be picked up four, eight or twelve years later, as if not a day had passed since the last phone call or e-mail.

Tamera Luzzatto was one of those friends. She had served as Hillary Clinton's chief of staff during her eight years in the US Senate. During the 2008 campaign, we were introduced by a mutual friend, Howard Paster, and had ridden its emotional Cortes waves through heartbreaking losses and ecstatic victories back then and in subsequent years.

So, when Tamera called and asked me to meet with Dan Schwerin, Hillary's speechwriter, my answer was "absolutely." A week or two later, in early March 2013, we chatted briefly over the phone and then met for coffee. We talked about the pathways to prosperity ranging from increasing consumer purchasing power to tax reforms that repatriated revenue held overseas by corporations, from hiring the unemployed to focusing on marketable skills that led to family-supporting careers.

My notes from that first conversation touched on two themes that would persist in various forms and formats, at least for me, for the next four years. I urged him to consider doing "not a single speech but a series of inserts aimed at a specific audience—the blue collar, working class workforce. They're always listening. And no one ever speaks to them." And I suggested that, in order to reconnect with these marginalized Americans, it was best to have those conversations in small, intimate settings where Secretary Clinton could keep asking, "How can we make your lives better?"

Within days, Schwerin and I were exchanging e-mails about the unemployed, the employment to population ratio, the labor movement, UCubed and public private partnerships. Sections of speech drafts and my suggestions were exchanged. And like in case of a fight club, you could not talk about it—complete silence and absolute discretion were the price of participation. And both of us knew what was at stake.

Just weeks after leaving the State Department, Sherwin was part of a six-person staff that Secretary Clinton set up in Washington, DC, to handle her scheduling and travel, craft her speeches and deflect media inquiries about running for president. While there were hundreds, if not thousands, of experts who pined for an invitation to submit thoughts and ideas to Schwerin and others, the office was not a precursor to another presidential campaign but a mini-idea factory.

By late May or early June, Sherwin sent me an e-mail with a series of statements and assertions that would drive a major speech or series of speeches by Secretary Clinton. Its thrust was more political—big economic trends and their impact on Americans' jobs and daily lives—and was more focused on a brighter future. But the crux of the exercise was global competition, investing in America's people, getting the private and public sectors working together and ending the gridlock.

My nine-page response began with an overarching theme that, four years later, would find a faint, an almost imperceptible echo in an acceptance speech. But, for me, the theme always held the premise behind, and promise of, a Hillary Clinton presidency:

> "We are a nation of builders. From the young couple putting together an IKEA bed to the ironworkers who topped off the One World Trade Center, from the entrepreneur finding financing for a lean start-up to the nurse managing digital health records, we are a nation of builders.
>
> Across the globe, we are admired for what we have built—the Saturn V rocket that took men to the moon, the Internet that connects us all, the massive farms that feed a hungry world, a system of land-grant colleges that became world class research facilities, an interstate highway system … a vast rail network … a spider web of airline routes and the cars, trains and jets that ply them.
>
> And yet, we built something less concrete, far more abstract and all too precious. We built a transcontinental republic where the people rule. We built an enduring democracy that our doubters and detractors said could never survive. And we built it to withstand the vagaries of time, the imperfections of its original compromises, the challenges that each new generation confronts, the attack of enemies here at home and abroad and the periodic calamities that nature and man might visit on our people.

This last decade damaged us. Hurricanes, tornadoes, earthquakes have ravaged our cities and towns. A financial meltdown and persistent joblessness have altered our economy. Our politics grew toxic and dysfunctional.

And yet, we are a nation of builders. It is time that we draw up new plans, invent new products and processes, reorganize and retrain our workforce, sharpen and shine our tools and get our Nation back to work building a new economy and rebuilding our democratic institutions."

While written as if text for a speech, the words never passed muster. That's not how Hillary Clinton spoke, and it was not what her audiences expected to hear. But it was very much what the jobless and working class families wanted to hear. And that point was made again and again in the rest of the memo.

"Can we ever be satisfied with a jobless recovery? Can we wait on the invisible hand—or foot, as the case may be—to hit the accelerator? Or can we come together to build a new, vibrant and sustainable economy?

Our challenge is not simply an economic one; it is a political one. We cannot be nation builders if our only tool is a hammer and we use it to beat our opponents senseless. At some point, the lumps—and I've taken and given my fair share—ought to tell us this is not working. And neither are enough of our people.

And therein lies our greatest challenge: how do we put aside the shibboleths and search for solutions? Together? Business and labor? Republican, Democrat and Independent? Black, Latino, Asian and Caucasian?

We start by recognizing that across the table, across the street, across the state line is another American who loves this country as much as we do. And we decide—as Americans have always tried to decide—to find common ground where common sense and common decency find common cause.

That space—perhaps, limited in time and focused on but a single issue—is built on trust, respect and recognition that pure adamancy, animosity and antagonism leads us nowhere. And we have an obligation to lead."

Clearly, I had no future as a speechwriter. I could—and did—warn Sherwin off two concepts that would prove disastrous for any Democratic presidential candidate. The first idea came from two economists at MIT's Sloan School of Management regarding hollowing out. I called their 19-step action plan an "assisted suicide pact" for any Democratic leader—just try to explain how to rapidly reduce wages by repealing minimum-wage laws, unemployment insurance, health benefits, prevailing wages and long-term contracts to a union audience.

Second, there was a pean to smart trade deals like the proposed Trans Pacific Partnership. That, too, was shot down by describing the TPP as "NAFTA on steriods" to most union members. "Pressing for the TPP was part of the secretary of states' job description," I added. "But as a private citizen, HRC has the option of calling for more openness (in negotiations). Raising the bar on expectations of what a fair trade deal might entail and addressing job loss arguments directly enables her to press for (even better) results . . . the more supportive she is of TPP, the more the business community will applaud and the more loudly labor will object."

It became clear to me that what I was responding to were excerpts from policy papers produced by the Hamilton Project, a Wall-Street-financed think-tank housed at the Brookings Institution.[24] It was named after Alexander Hamilton, the first Treasury Secretary, and its board directors and executive directors read like a list of *who's who* of the revolving door between the federal government, Goldman Sachs and similar financial firms.

To combat the economic elites' policy suggestions, I reverted to an idea that even Alexander Hamilton abhorred—democracy.

"What's different today is that democracy has given way to adamancy. It's my way or the highway. And that's not healthy for either [any] party or any politician. Because it means a monarchy of one must decide everything.

We can take principled stands and we can fight tooth and nail for our positions, but when it comes time to act or enact, we must find common ground. Compromise isn't a dirty word. It is what sustains our democracy—it is what makes majority rule work. And, if you don't believe in majority rule, you really don't believe in our democracy.

'Let's vote' isn't a battle cry. It is what we do as Americans. It is how We, the People, decide on our collective future …

And by insisting on super-majorities to address every piece of legislation and every nomination, by making it more difficult to exercise our right to vote, by allowing vast flows of money to influence the votes being cast and the language of our laws, we demean, diminish and debilitate our democracy.

Is that what we really want for America? Less democracy? And more monarchies of one? Frankly, I thought that issue was settled in 1776."

I was writing for an audience of one. Hopefully. And it wasn't Schwerin. My audience was an honorary member of the Machinists, a former secretary of state and, within a couple of years, perhaps, a presidential candidate.

On the political spectrum of the Democratic Party, the Machinists were about as far left of center as the Hamilton Project was far right. To let their lobbying efforts go unanswered, even if the audience for those speeches were executives of Goldman Sachs and Solomon Brothers, seemed, somehow, disloyal. So I began pushing my work products through as many doors as possible and kept searching for allies at every turn.

CHAPTER 24

THE INVISIBLES

I was working as a forklift mechanic and began experiencing many health problems. After shoulder, knee and hand surgery, among other injuries, I realized I would not be able to make it to retirement. I went back to school to become an elementary school teacher ... I had to resign my daytime job to perform my student teacher program. Now I am in debt and cannot find a job.

John's Unemployment Story

The concept behind the "invisibles" was neither novel nor new. Having watched hundred hours of taped interviews of the men and women who raced toward the sounds of the sirens while others were fleeing on September 11—at the World Trade Towers and the Pentagon—I knew that it was their strength, skill and courage that gave us hope on that terrible day. I knew their names.[25] I had memorized their faces in the process of editing *Everyday Heroes*, a documentary about their selfless acts of courage.

I had met their significant others at its first screening and watched as their never-before-shared stories brought tears to their loved one's eyes.

I had also written a Labor Day message for Tom Buffenbarger based on those heartrending stories:

> "ESU officers Mark Demarco and Bill Beaury directed folks down the stairwells surviving the collapse of Tower Two and then riding the rubble down in Tower One. NYPD officer Jose Rodriguez ducked falling bodies and gave last rites to Father Judge. Ambulance driver Joseph Conzo, after finding his way out from under the pile, helped injured firefighters and WTC employees into ferry boats manned by men like Jim Silecchia.

> At the Pentagon, Virginia state trooper Michael Middleton raced to help his fellow officer Myrlin Wimbish search for survivors. These two troopers—one white, one black—made it to the fifth floor before the heat and smoke drove them back. Wimbish ended up carrying Middleton outside where he collapsed with thermal burns to his lungs. At Ground Zero, many would come down with what they called the [*World Trade Center*]*cough* from inhaling a toxic stew of dust for days on end.

> Some draped massive chains over their shoulders. Others brought torches and tips to cut steel. Still more, thousands more, carried little more than a union card. They knew exactly where their duty lay: at the epicenter of the tragedy.

> In Virginia, Pennsylvania and New York, the 'invisibles'—the men and women who work an eight-hour shift, who work with their hands, who raise their families in neighborhoods where network news cameras never go—started to just show up.

> Guys like Hector Ramirez drove his train into Cortland Station and, disobeying orders from his dispatchers, stopped to pick

up hundreds stranded beneath the World Trade Center. His was the last train to leave the station before steel beams smashed through to the tunnels.

Julia Martinez and Margaret Espinoza pushed wheel-chair-bound kids past the falling bodies and debris. Then, when the dust clogged the chair's electric motors, they carried these students to safety on their backs.

Sean Woods, Bob Benesh and Pete Creegan hand carried chunks of steel girders to clear paths for rescue workers; Mary Stein grabbed her lab coat and medical kit to dress wounds; Pete D'Ancona used a steel girder to pry cement blocks off a fellow firefighter."

These "invisibles" were America's heart and soul and sinew. And Hillary Clinton knew it. As the senator from New York, she walked the streets with the city's mayor, Rudy Giuliani, near where the Twin Towers had stood side by side. She sought health care for those who worked on the pile or fought the fires at the Pentagon. She understood exactly who the invisibles were and she spoke about them with emotion and caring.

During an early trip to New Hampshire in 2007, she had listed the "invisibles" that a callous GOP president could not see: the hard working parent, the first responder, a soldier returning from combat, a child sitting in a failing school, a single mom who needs quality child care. "For six long years," she said, "they have been invisible. Well, they're not invisible to us. They're not invisible to me."

Her speech to the Democratic Party's "100 Club" Dinner was unforgettable. It was one of the reasons that I had fought so hard during the 2008 contests, one of the reasons I readily accepted the chance to work with her speechwriter six years later, one of the reasons I produced a series of four memos for Tamera Luzzatto, the first of which was titled "The Invisibles' Momentum" and was dated August 29, 2013. Its central message was,

"Having watched the 2008 campaign closely, then-Senator Clinton proved that she did not only want to be the president, she also ran to make progress on an agenda that she had worked on for decades, an agenda focused on her 'invisibles.' She connected with—and drew strength from—those who never would walk the halls of power. Over time, her fight became their fight.

Her "invisibles" have vanished from the airwaves but they have not disappeared. They constitute the Clinton Factor—a broad swath of working class voters that would support her should she run again and, if she decided against another run, would listen carefully to her suggestion about what must be done by the next president and who that should be. Their loyalty to her was earned in the hardest way possible—the crucibles called Ohio, Texas, Pennsylvania and West Virginia. By speaking directly to their lives and not giving up on them as so many others had, Hillary won more than their votes. She won their hearts.

And yet, the intervening years devastated her "invisibles." They were hammered by the Great Recession, financially and emotionally. Unable to find jobs when laid off, they saw their house values plummet, their bank accounts and IRAs drain away and their kids' aspirations crater. But the most painful experience was that no one in power seemed to give a damn about what was happening to them."

Her "invisibles" will long remember what they endured. Their households know, intimately, the damage done. And they know how many friends, family members and neighbors fell out of the middle class. For them, the Great Recession never really ended. And the celebrations over declining unemployment rates were not just premature but a cruel, monthly hoax perpetrated by politicians of both parties.

"These working class families—black, brown and white—are waiting to hear what their Hillary has to say. They will wait to see what she intends to do. And they will hold out the hope—and perhaps act on that hope—that she will decide to fight for them again."

No response was expected. None was forthcoming. That's not how it works in the pre-announcement period of a nascent presidential campaign. Unsolicited strategy memos are a dime a dozen. Their value comes not from who receives them but on whether or not they are shared with the ultimate decision-maker or becomes grist for senior advisors. A cone of silence often descends over those deliberations, particularly when a potential candidate is still deciding to make the race.

Several months later, I refocused my arguments on the 2014 midterm elections that were but a year away and would see the electorate shrink by 40 million voters from its 2012 presidential high water mark. This time I asked,

"What are the Democrats offering their base vote? Reopening government, keeping the individual mandate and controlling Syrian chemical weapons, as important as those actions are, will not mobilize marginalized Democratic voters. By ignoring the demand for jobs, a growing economy and relief from the price increases imposed by grocers, insurers and utilities, those Democratic incumbents and challengers are left to argue: Cross our hearts. We're better than those other clowns.

That's a policy prescription for losing control of the United States Senate, expanding the GOP margin in the House and re-electing the Republican governors who won in 2010," I predicted and then dove into the heart of the challenge facing Hillary.

"And whether or not Secretary Clinton campaigns next fall is immaterial. No one person can alter the dynamics where 40 million voters stay home. What she can and should do is encourage her friends to craft a message that moves Democratic leaning stay-at-homes to go vote and then persuade incumbents and challengers to adopt that message.

What is important to understand is that the results in 2014 could make governing from 2017 to 2025 nearly impossible. It's not de jure control of the Congress by Republicans that worries me; de facto control does. Lose a few seats and the Neanderthals become more powerful and brazen."

To me, 2014 was a laboratory to test messages and touch crucial constituencies. And I argued, again vainly, that Hillary Clinton's "invisibles" ought to be her primary audience. They were still hurting, and no one was even paying them lip service.

CHAPTER 25

AMERICA'S NOT WORKING CLASS

I am now 57 years old and have been insulted by a couple of businesses, asking me if I even know to use a computer. I am years away from Social Security and too old to be among the little graphic artist wanna-be bunnies who work for nothing and know nothing with no real work ethic! I am tired of being out of work and tired of being age discriminated against ...

Karen's Unemployment Story

On the first Friday of each month starting in January 2007, Leo Hindery, Jr., had e-mailed his analysis of the BLS monthly unemployment report to senators, members of Congress, reporters, congressional staff, labor union and business leaders. He was a major contributor to Democratic campaigns, particularly senate incumbents and challengers, and his generosity meant he would be taken seriously. He was also a big idea guy writing about corporate responsibility, economic policy, trade and job creation. Having written economic policy papers and speeches for the Edwards and Obama campaigns, Hindery had enormous credibility to challenge the government's narrowly defined unemployment rate.

Using the BLS's own numbers and clear explanations of who was included and who was excluded from their *official* announcements about U-3, the headline driving rate that so underreported America's joblessness, Hindery demonstrated that the *real* unemployment number and the *raw* number of unemployed were, consistently, twice as high (or more) as the government's approximation.

"As we note each month," Hindery's e-mails patiently explained, "BLS's Unemployment Rate does *not* reflect Real Unemployment because fundamentally BLS counts only those persons who are actively looking for employment." His November 2013 e-mail continued as follows:

"BLS does *not* include among unemployed persons (i.e., the 'numerator') the 9.8 million workers in total who are either 'marginally attached' or, much more numerous, 'part-time-of-necessity', as follows:

a. **'Marginally attached workers,'** of whom there are now **1.3 million**, are workers who 'while wanting and available for jobs, have not searched for work specifically in the past four weeks but have searched for work in the past twelve months.' Included among them are **0.7 million 'discouraged workers'** who did not look for work at all because 'they believe there are no jobs available or none for which they would qualify.'

b. **'Part-time-of-necessity (or PTN) workers,'** of whom there are now **7.7 million**, are workers who are unable to find full-time jobs or who've had their hours cut back.

BLS does *not* include in the civilian labor force (i.e., the 'denominator') marginallyattached workers (although it does include PTN workers)."

Each month, Hindery provided a summary that showed how the number of *real* unemployed persons decreased or increased. He also highlighted how his *real* unemployment rate grew or ebbed from the month before. His most provocative paragraph, however, came last:

"In addition to the 20.6 million Real Unemployed Persons [on] October 31, there were another 3.3 million workers who, while saying they want jobs, have not looked for work in the past twelve months. Solely because they haven't looked, these workers are not included among the marginally attached workers; if included, then November's Real Unemployment Rate of 13.1% increases to 14.9%."

In November 2013, the BLS estimate of the number of unemployed Americans was 10.8 million—13.1 million *fewer* than Hindery's all-in number. The *official* unemployment rate was 6.9 percent—8.0 percent *lower* than his all-in rate.

The point that Hindery kept making dealt with how BLS, by manipulating fractions and percentages, were making themselves and the political leaders to whom they reported feel good but failed to capture the pain and angst the unemployed and their families were still experiencing. By leaving 15.5 million of marginally attached, part-time-out-of necessity and those who hadn't looked in the last year out of the denominator, BLS pushed the unemployment rate down into single digits.

By excluding marginally attached workers and the growing number of Americans who simply abandoned the workforce entirely from the denominator, the BLS kept the denominator steady. Besides, no one seemed to care about the millions who had prematurely retired or stayed in academia longer.

Good for politicians. Not so good for the jobless. Their extended unemployment benefits were tied directly to the *official* unemployment rate. As it fell, the number of weeks they received $300 in extended unemployment benefits also declined.

As bad as that was, it was before the Republican-led Congress got into the act. Even as Hindery's e-mail landed, GOP leaders were expected to chop 1.3 million Americans off the unemployment rolls in January 2014. Another 1.9 million were to face a similar fate the following June.

As Christmas approached, the *real* unemployment number stood at 20.6 million and another 3.5 million Americans wanted to work but hadn't looked in the past year. Those 24.1 million unemployed, underemployed and uncounted Americans exceeded the entire population of Texas!

Members of Congress who branded the unemployed as "hobos" had Texas-sized egos but, to borrow a phrase from the Lone Star State, they were "all hat and no cattle . . . all talk and no action." But UCubed had been working on a plan to harass the worst offenders, the ones who believed they were untouchable politically, the ones who felt they could attack the jobless with impunity.

UCubed was intent on a two-track strategy.

First, it planned to run a national issue-oriented campaign for much of 2014. Called "America's NOT Working Class," its primary objective was to expand our reach in the 22 states where 101 Republican members of Congress had won with between 54 percent and 62 percent of the votes cast in 2012. That targeting universe meant they were neither the most competitive marginal districts nor were they completely and hopelessly lost. But they were districts where there were significant numbers of mostly working class Democrats who generated 38 percent to 46 percent of the turnout in midterm elections.

Those 101 congressional districts were found in states where UCubed already had significant numbers of Facebook activists. They were also in states where GOP governors like Brian Sandoval (NV), Scott Walker (WI), Rick Snyder (MI), John Kasich (OH), Tom Corbett (PA), Rick Scott (FL), Jan Brewer (AZ), Nathan Deal (GA), Bill Haslam (TN) and Rick Perry (TX) had run as job creators in 2010 but failed to produce results. On the federal level, GOP senators like Mitch McConnell (KY), Saxby Chambliss (GA), Lamar Alexander (TN) and John Cornyn (TX) had held the unemployed hostage to their own austerity agendas.

On the Democratic side, those 22 states covered Senators Dick Durbin (IL), Tom Udall (NM), Jeff Merkley (OR), John Warner (VA), Mark Udall (CO), Carl Levin (MI), Al Franken (MN) and North Carolina Senator Kay Hagan's reelection campaigns and incumbent Governors Jerry Brown (CA), John Hickenloper (CO), Mark Dayton (MN), Andrew Cuomo (NY), John Kitzhaber (OR) and Pat Quinn (IL). All had voted for unemployment benefits, food stamps and COBRA discounts for the jobless or had tried to turn around their state's economy.

The 101 GOP members of Congress had provided 70 percent of the votes intending to keep the government closed and default on the national debt just months earlier. They hailed from districts that Democratic incumbents and challengers would occasionally visit but seldom choose as places to expend their limited resources. And yet, the money those GOP congressmen raised (and often did not spend on their own campaigns) always flowed toward defeating Democrats at the top of the ticket.[26] So, our plan was to harass them enough to keep some of those millions at home.

The second part of the UCubed plan entailed recruiting 50,000 new Facebook activists from those districts, entertaining them with humorous posts, memes and videos, and then encouraging them and their all-important *friends of fans'* to Get Out To Vote.[27] Unlike our 2012 campaign, this one would take direct aim at the Tea Party and its gang-that-couldn't-shoot-straight approach to resolving America's job crisis. Without endorsing or advocating for any specific candidate, the campaign would remind voters of the Tea Party's theatrics and how they had consistently backfired.

"Frankly, this is a crazy, wild ass strategy," I admitted to both Tom Buffenbarger and Leo Hindery. "It pits us against the 46 Tea Party groups that signed on to the blueprint to shut down the government in order to defund Obamacare. It essentially targets the most radical Tea Party members of Congress, senators and governors with no expectation of defeating any of them. And it does so on a shoe-string budget."

Unbelievably, they bought into the idea. So did others. Eventually.

Democratic strategists and campaign technicians never did. They were firmly footed in the old way of doing business and never understood the power of Facebook to move messages across the nation inexpensively. They never understood that UCubed represented an army of volunteers who with a click of the *like* or *share* button could send our message on to 285 of their friends. Nor did they grasp that such a personal endorsement had the power to persuade and turn out the marginalized, working class Democrats that UCubed recruited.

Instead the powers-that-be were committed to fighting the last war, with the same tactics that had failed them in that war, and permitted their direct mail and online fundraising operations to pound away at the idea that Democrats faced another disastrous defeat in 2014. To those apostles of defeat, it was 2010 again and the GOP wave was rushing toward them. When 25 million Americans could not find a full-time job or were so discouraged they hadn't looked for a year, hearing those political vendors caterwauling about how awful things were was more than disheartening. It was damn depressing, anger-provoking and totally counterproductive.

When America's *not* working class numbered 103 million, even the dullest hack ought to have been able to find a way to turn their economic peril into a potent message. For it was just sitting there waiting for someone, anyone to use. So UCubed did.

According to the BLS, that 103 million included 11 million unemployed and 92 million who were "not in the labor force." That same BLS, whose unemployment numbers were so questionable, unhelpfully explained that "many who are not in the labor force are going to school or are retired. Family responsibilities keep others out of the labor force." What the BLS did not include were the 7 million part-time workers caught up in slack work or unfavorable business conditions—their words, not mine.

"This painfully slow economic recovery," I wrote for a broadcast e-mail, "has had a direct impact on each one of those 110 million Americans. They worry about their own and their family's future ... every day. And all they want America to be is ascendant once again." For the next nine months, that would be the mantra for UCubed and its Facebook activists.

CHAPTER 26

ASSAULT ON THE CHAMELEONS

Nowadays my days are filled with endless job searches, phone calls from collection agencies and unbearable levels of stress. If this is supposed to be the American Dream, this certainly isn't what I had in mind.

Michael's Unemployment Story

Four years after launching the Union of Unemployed, its Facebook posts and photos were reaching 1.7 million folks per week. It had grown to 175,000 activists and expected to add another 50,000 before the 2104 midterm elections.

In the intervening years, the *official* unemployment rate had dropped from 10 percent to 6.7 percent. The broadest measure of joblessness—the infamous U-6—declined from 17.1 percent to 13.1 percent. And Hindery's number of *real* unemployed was now 24 million, a significant improvement over the 30.8 million of unemployed, underemployed and uncounted in 2010.

Seeing 6.7 million Americans return to work was encouraging. But it was impossible to cheer when 24 million men and women were still looking for full-time work. It was political folly to ignore the increases in the "not in the labor force" category since 2010. That BLS number would be highlighted each month by the *Drudge Report* as it grew from 83.9 million to over 100 million during President Obama's two terms.

To those who cared to look closely, America faced a jobs crisis even if *official* Washington did not want to deal with that all-too-inconvenient fact. There were deep pockets of joblessness in Black, Latino and blue collar communities, communities that traditionally gave significant support to Democratic candidates. Such joblessness was so pervasive and so persistent that it was becoming structural unemployment. Harkening back to Senator Bob Casey's comment that the "unemployed don't vote," that level of joblessness—and hopelessness—drove down voter turnout as folks just gave up.

In the 2014 midterm elections, when 40 million registered voters who had voted two years previously could not be bothered with going to the polls, the balance of power shifted toward the Republican Party. So, any decrease in enthusiasm among Democratic voters because of economic conditions had the potential to create a wave election. In early 2014, another tsunami was building just over the horizon.

There were, however, early warning signs. In mid-March, a special election was held in Florida. Alex Sink, the Democratic congressional nominee, lost because 158,000 voters stayed home. That represented a 47 percent drop in turnout from the 2012 presidential election in the district.

But there was another and equally insidious factor. The *official* unemployment rate in Pinellas County had dropped from 12 percent in 2010 to 5.7 percent in January 2014.[28] So Sink focused on breaking the gridlock in Washington, flood insurance, Medicare and social security, veterans, growing small business, wasteful government spending and fixing Obamacare—the top seven issues on her campaign website. Words like "unemployment" and "joblessness" were nowhere to be found. In a poll-driven, television-ad-heavy campaign aimed at an increasingly smaller slice of undecided voters, that was now to be expected. Why talk about the "invisibles" when they were unlikely to vote?

That, in a nutshell, was the Democratic dilemma. The drop off was owing to the dropouts.

When 47 percent of those who had voted just 15 months before decided to stay home, Sink was sunk. Sadly, that pattern—lower turnout among traditional Democratic constituencies—would be repeated over and over again in 2014 and, most devastatingly, in 2016.

For that 5.7 percent unemployment rate was a false flag. It did not capture the *real* unemployment rate nor did it include the dropouts from the workforce. And it led Democratic strategists to ignore the voters they really needed: "America's NOT Working Class."

Not so UCubed. By the end of March, it had added 25,000 fans. Included in that growth spurt were 15,000 Facebook activists who lived in the targeted 101 congressional districts. It was creating a covert army of activists in those deep red districts, an army that already had 4 million friends and family members most of whom lived in those same 22 states.

Equally important, Glenn Totten and I thought we had figured out a way to drive a wedge between the local Tea Party activists and the GOP establishment. To us, the alliance between older, whiter, more affluent middle class voters who supported the Tea Party and the more corporate, country club Republican Party led by Mitch McConnell and John Boehner seemed to be cracking. The fissures were microscopic. But primaries in Texas, Georgia, Idaho, North Carolina and Kentucky were expanding those cracks.

Our animated imagery was being designed to remind Tea Party voters about what they most disliked about their own member of Congress—that they toed the Tea Party line back home but looked out for "Numero Ono" once elected. And, like a chameleon, they changed their colors to match their political environment.

Changing their colors from their yellow don't-tread-on-me flag, the trademark of the Tea Party, to red, white and blue, the colors of patriotism, was easy once the animated chameleon was created. So, too, was changing its color to green (with dollar signs) to convey their greed. One other biological fact—chameleons have hyper-ballistic tongues that shoot out of their mouths to twice their body length—made their animated capture of wads of cash both disgusting and thoroughly entertaining. Cartoon humor still worked to make a political point.

As the eight animated episodes of "Chamo the Chameleon" were being generated, UCubed kept growing, domestically and internationally. Each month, it reached 10.2 million folks in the United States, 440,000 in Canada and 1.6 million in 46 other countries. It engaged more than a half million Americans who liked, shared or commented on our posts. Another 90,000 fans were engaged across the globe.

In June 2014, UCubed had 218,000 Facebook activists and engaged 600,000 of them each month. By comparison, *Ready for Hillary*, the political action committee that was a forerunner of the Clinton campaign, had nine times as many fans but only one-third of our engagement level. The US Chamber of Commerce had 347,000 fans but engaged only 4,200 per month. The AFL-CIO had 134,000 fans and engaged 20,000. In terms of engagement, the real measure of a page's effectiveness, UCubed had cracked the code even as Facebook had begun to change its algorithms.

By Labor Day, UCubed exceeded its goal of 50,000 new Facebook activists in the 101 targeted GOP congressional districts. I had researched the 990s—federal filings for nonprofits that provided both donor and expenditure data—and the Federal Election Committee reports for the 46 Tea Party organizations that had signed onto the strategy to shut down the government and block increases in America's debt ceiling. My findings showed a multi-million dollar effort to derail our democracy in order to defund Obamacare. The so-called grassroots movement that the Tea Party touted was really an astroturf effort financed by a half dozen or so billionaires and their family members. And those simple, incontestable factoids— who gave what to whom and when—were turned into a series of memes UCubed called the "Tee Hee Hee Partee" posts. The Tea Partiers patrons' paeans to patriotism were a joke, a bad joke. They were only protecting their assets.

So over the next 65 days, UCubed spent $65,000 and reached 10.7 million Facebook users. Our memes and animated cartoons often went viral spiking our cumulative daily total reach to more than 34 million and our cumulative daily total impressions to 63 million!

Our Facebook-centric strategy generated 260,000 fans—more fans than all but four senate or gubernatorial campaigns (Democrats Wendy Davis, Al Franken, Cory Booker and Republican Greg Abbot). UCubed level of engagement doubled that of 19 Democratic statewide campaigns. In 14 more states, the UCubed level engagement with its own activists represented a 50 percent to 75 percent increase over and above the Democratic candidate's own level of engagement.

UCubed went where others feared to tread. Its "Tee Hee Hee Partee" posts, photos and videos reached 10 million Facebook users and its humorous videos, starring Chamo the Chameleon, were served up to 6.4 million Facebook users. Most impressive, UCubed helped cut the margins of victory by 5.8 percent, on average, in 10 of the targeted districts and even saw one congressional district flip from the Republicans to the Democrats in what otherwise proved to be a GOP tidal wave.

Chamo the Chameleon kept swallowing wads of cash with the nation's capitol in the background, voting with the corporate interests that funded its campaigns and turning his back on the true-believers who had rallied to the Tea Party. His coloring matched the environment—the green shade of dollar bills.

CHAPTER 27

HIT WITH A TWO-BY-FOUR

I will be a 99er right before this Memorial Day ... I go to three food banks each month to get by. I've never had to do that. Necessities are becoming luxuries for me. I have no medical anymore—I couldn't afford it after the COBRA expired. I'm two months behind on my mortgage and after I pay it I have nothing left for all my bills. I called my representative who told me they didn't vote for the recent bill to help 99ers because it had no hope [of passage]. I don't know how these people sleep at night. I know I can't.

Michele's Unemployment Story

Even as UCubed was battling the Tea Party and its GOP allies with humor, I was engaged in a serious e-mail exchange with Hillary Clinton's speechwriter. He had asked for my thoughts on a couple of speeches that Hillary would give in Iowa and Kentucky to support Democrats running for the Senate.

My initial e-mail argued that her target audience should be white working class Democrats, particularly women with less than a college education. Secretary Clinton should talk about the micro-economics of paying utility bills and insurance premiums, buying gas and groceries, meeting monthly rent and car loan obligations—all the while working harder and seeing the American Dream getting smaller and more distant for many, and simply slipping out of reach for others.

By recognizing that they had tried to build a better life in the face of the worst economic storms in 75 years, by acknowledging their sacrifices and the damage done to their hopes, she could lay the groundwork for describing who, exactly, had delayed and diminished their dreams.

Schwerin's response came within 15 minutes. He, essentially, replied that mine was not a great answer for middle class families. My response, written well past midnight, was,

> "First, we're not talking about middle class families. That's what working class Democrats aspire to become. But right now all discussions of the middle class just talk right past the target audience.
>
> These are folks who rallied to HRC because they saw in her their champion. Just because they never went to college did not mean they were clueless. Some might say, in retrospect, they saw through the hype and counted on Clinton.
>
> So they're listening carefully to what she has to say about their lives. And their lives are hard, up early, work all day and no one in government gives them a second thought. Or understands what it's like to live on the margins."

My e-mail then shifted to a less antagonistic tone. Its second point focused on the fact that working class Democrats weren't looking for a silver bullet:

> "They're too shrewd to buy into the idea that life's going to get so much easier if only we'd pass HR1010 or HR1000. They've

got kids and grand kids and they've been around the block a few times.

Instead, what they want is for someone to tell them the truth: HRC sees what they face—higher prices, harder times, heftier debts and a fear that something has gone terribly wrong. And one bill, one idea, one initiative is not the answer.

There are more challenges to meet than there are days in a year. We've put many of them off for decades. And we've let the few dictate to the many what can never be done."

Never a tangential point, what I was driving at had more to do with how Americans governed themselves than with the immediate issue of writing a campaign speech or two. And that point would be made more eloquently in the months ahead.

"The only antidote to government by the few is government by the many—a democratic revival," I argued. "THEY are the answer. The government is THEM. And only THEIR votes and THEIR reengagement can switch us from the wrong track to the right track."

"Democracy isn't a fire and forget exercise," I reminded Schwerin, "It's about THEM digging in, being determined, driving to the finish line. Challenging white working class Democrats, particularly women, to work harder than they've ever worked to make government respond to THEIR needs is her call to action."

Sherwin's answer, which arrived near dawn, stunned me: "Doesn't a national leader need to talk to everyone, not just a demo slice?" One-half of Hillary Clinton's votes in the 2008 primaries and caucuses had just been relegated to a demographic slice of the electoral pie.

And yet, to his credit, Hillary's speeches for Allyson Grimes and Gary Peters included appeals to blue collar, working class families—those Hillary Clinton Democrats. And the national media noticed, including some of its most observant reporters. E. J. Dionne did an entire column on it. Amy Chozick, a perennial adversary from the *New York Times*, argued that those working class votes would be her strength.

Demo slice or strength? That question would remain unanswered for another year . . . or two.

As a peace offering, I sent Schwerin an article from Leo Hindery, Jr., that appeared in the *Huffington Post* on Labor Day 2014. It talked about America's *real* unemployment crisis and his six years of tracking what the BLS included (and excluded) from its monthly reports. Hindery, too, was troubled by the Democrats' attitudes:

> "Across this nation, many Democratic candidates and their campaigns have the sense that they are about to be beaten. And in truth, virtually every political pundit, electoral model and poll has them losing majorities in the House and Senate, albeit in each case narrowly.
>
> And 'narrowly' is the key word.
>
> If these Democratic candidates would shake off their senses of gloom and doom, they could excite the electorate with the prospects of un-divided government and of real statesmen leading the Senate, House of Representatives and National Governors Association."

Hindery's piece ended with a shout-out to UCubed. "At the Union of Unemployed, my friend Rick Sloan is doing the right thing. He has recruited over 225,000 Facebook fans, including 50,000 from 101 deeply red Congressional Districts. His efforts are now reaching up to 4.8 million folks per week with aggressive messaging and indisputable facts."

"In less than nine weeks we will see if the Real Unemployed either rally to Democratic candidates or Republican candidates. But if Mr. Sloan is right, these 23.2 million American workers could alter the course of American history and deliver a resounding rebuke to whose who've made them suffer unduly for nearly six long years."

The stunning stone-deafness of Democratic candidates, their failure to appeal directly to the 23.2 million unemployed Americans and their inexplicable failure to exploit new ways of reaching them would soon come home to roost. The results would be devastating. Would they finally wake up? Would those results be the two-by-four that knocked some sense into Democratic message makers and candidates?

One could only hope so, but I wasn't counting on it.

CHAPTER 28

REPUBLICAN INFRASTRUCTURE

I am 25 years old … I am one of 190,000 teachers laid off … The United States of America is being allowed to commit sepuku, ritual suicide. If we turn our backs on people like me, who have striven so hard to be the best person I can be, then we turn our backs on the future, the present and the past.

A Florida Teacher's Unemployment Story

Not since Pearl Harbor had so few Americans turned out for a midterm election. According to the US Election Project, only 83.2 million citizens bothered to vote—a decrease of 46 million from two years earlier! And that riptide of disinterested citizens handed President Barack Obama and the Democratic Party their second massive midterm election defeat in a row.

Republicans won control of the US Senate, 54 to 46, by winning a net nine seats. In the House of Representatives, the GOP caucus grew to 247—29 votes more than the simple majority needed to pass legislation—and the largest Republican margin since 1928.

But the damage did not stop there.

Republicans picked up two more governors' offices, bringing their total to 31. And they controlled 68 state legislative bodies. The bright side, if there was one, was that Democrats won 121 more state representative and state senator seats than in 2012.

Voter turnout slumped by 36 percent. Whites made up 75 percent of the turnout, blacks were 12 percent, Latinos were 8 percent and Asians were 3 percent. Millennials were 13 percent, down 6 percentage points from 2012. White working class voters made up 36 percent of the turnout and voted nearly two to one Republican (64 percent to 34 percent).

According to the exit polls, those who worked full time for pay—the only published question that dealt with employment status—were 60 percent of all voters. What UCubed had been calling "America's NOT working class" was, consequently, 40 percent of the turnout. Nine months later, when the US Census issued its report on the 2014 election, it confirmed that the unemployed and "not in labor force" totaled 36 million out of the 92 million of voters who said they went to the polls. Those two categories represented 39 percent of the turnout.

In the census survey, the unemployed numbered only 7.6 million and 2.3 million reported voting in the congressional elections. So 30 percent of them voted. The rest had, basically, given up on their democracy. From a political standpoint, the unemployed had come full circle. From not voting in 2006 to being the angriest voters of 2010 and from being integral to the Obama victories in 2008 and 2012, they had dropped out of the political process and dropped off the politicians' radar screens.

Despite this, the issues that mattered most to the unemployed were the dominant motivators for the electorate in 2014, according to the exit polls. The unemployed won the messaging war. Their issues dominated the opinions of the voters in 2014. More than three-quarters (78 percent) of all voters, according to the exit polls, said they were worried about economic conditions. Almost half (48 percent) said that life for the next generation would be worse than today. Only two in five (42 percent) thought Hillary Clinton would make a good president; 53 percent disagreed.

So, yes, Republicans won an impressive victory. At the same time, they created the infrastructure required to retake the White House in 2016.

Those 301 Republican senators and members of Congress controlled the investigative committees that would make "Benghazi" a household word and that, in due course, would demand access to Secretary Clinton's e-mails and those of her staff. The GOP austerity agenda would face repeated veto threats from the White House but President Obama never actually vetoed one of those bills until 2015.[29] And their drumbeat about ISIS, domestic terrorism and illegal immigration would fill the airwaves—and their social media accounts—for the next two years.

But that GOP infrastructure was more extensive than most Democratic strategists understood. In the 31 states with Republican governors, political patronage, legislative initiatives and regulatory rulings kept the campaign contributions flowing. State and county parties were flush, research and polling continued and organizational efforts, usually shut down between elections, kept the staff engaged. Thus, the spoils of political warfare were shared widely with the corporations and wealthy contributors who expected not just access, but results.

What few Democrats realized was that the costs of the new necessities of life—cable television, electric power, natural gas, cellular and internet service—were being jacked up by captive regulatory agencies, agencies dominated by appointees named by those GOP governors. The critical services many of the unemployment relied on—Medicaid, unemployment benefits, public schools—were seeing budget cuts that cascaded from the Congress down to the state legislatures dominated by Republicans.

In a way, the GOP infrastructure created a virtual power loop. Contributors received tax cuts, corporate welfare and friendly regulators willing to pass on higher costs to consumers. They had tangible incentives to keep contributing, and they did. Candidates and campaign committees collected half a billion dollars in contributions and reinvested them in building the party's infrastructure, expanding their messaging delivery platforms, their "Get Out The Vote" capabilities and preparing for the 2016 elections.

One of the GOP's most surprising investments during the 2014 election cycle was in Facebook. It was not at all obvious during the election but in the final days it proved decisive.

In late October, Facebook produced an online comparison of each statewide race—the senate and governors' contests, wherever one existed. They also did similar comparisons for each congressional district race. Once the election results were finalized, I analyzed Facebook's impact. It defied the odds.

In the 64 House races monitored by *The Cook Political Report*, the GOP won 76 percent of the Facebook fan battles. In the most competitive congressional races in the country, Republican candidates had more fans or "likes" than the Democratic candidates did. In the senate races, the GOP won 72 percent of the Facebook fan battles. The GOP won 69 percent of the head-to-head gubernatorial Facebook fan battles.

That might sound like I am belittling the Republican Party's achievement. My assessment is quite the contrary. While the number of fans—or *likes*—did not appear to have a direct bearing on the outcome of those contests, the number of fans did signify a sea change in how successful campaigns would approach Facebook in the future. Their fans' engagement levels, if UCubed's own engagement levels were any indication, would improve over time and, in at least one instance, would flip a contest at very little cost.

So, as a compulsive number cruncher, I dutifully compiled all the Facebook stats to compare them with what UCubed had done. What I found was astonishing. In the 64 most competitive House races, Republican candidates had 895,000 fans and the Democrats had 347,000 fans—an advantage of more than half a million. Engagement levels were minuscule except in three contests: Kyrsten Cinema (D-AZ) with 16,600 per week, Dan Boningo's 12,700 per week in his unsuccessful challenge to John Delaney (D-MD) and Mike Bost's 3,800 per week in his victory over Rep. Bill Enyart (D-IL). Most of the other losing candidates never broke the 1,000 engaged fans level per week.

In the gubernatorial contests, Democratic candidates had 1.5 million fans and engaged 345,000 per week. Republican candidates for governor had 2 million likes and engaged 380,000 per week. Not a huge difference. Except then I realized that half a million of those Democratic candidates' total fans and a third of their engagement came from one candidate: Wendy Davis, the losing Democratic gubernatorial nominee in Texas. Her opponent, Greg Abbott, only reduced the GOP totals by 400,000 fans and 82,000 engaged users. Democrats, outside of Texas, were getting beaten by 700,000 fans and by 86,000 engaged users each week.

That doesn't seem like much until you take into account the multiplier effect inherent in Facebook. Each engaged fan also had 200 to 300 Facebook friends or family members. That meant the Republican gubernatorial campaigns were reaching between 17 and 26 million *more* folks each week than the Democratic nominees were!

One state demonstrated the power of Facebook engagements: Maryland. There Anthony Brown, an African American, two-term lieutenant governor and a man with both an impressive combat record and years of public service, faced off against Larry Hogan, a real estate broker with virtually no name recognition and a slim public service record. Hogan won both the battle of the fans and engagement levels. Brown had 28,800 fans and engaged 3,100 of them per week; Hogan had 123,000 fans and engaged 30,200 of them per week. Hogan's stunning victory, a victory by 68,000 votes in a heavily Democratic state, was the biggest upset of the year and was due almost entirely to his dominance on Facebook.

In the US Senate races, GOP candidates also won the Facebook fan battles. By election day, Republicans had 2 million fans while Democrats had 1.4 million fans. But Democrats won the engagement fights—or thought they did if they gave it any thought at all. Democratic candidates engaged 335,000 each week; Republican candidates for Senate had 186,000 engaged partisans each week.

However, two Democratic candidates drew the lion's share of that Facebook activity. Senators Al Franken (MN) and Corey Booker (NJ) had 737,000 of those 1.4 million fans and they accounted for 111,000 of those engaged weekly. Franken won by 200,000 votes; Booker won by 244,000 votes.

Still, when you looked at the highest profile races, three stand out. In Georgia's open seat, Democrat Michelle Nunn lost the Facebook battle by 37,100 fans to David Purdue who won the election by 201,000 votes. In Arkansas, Democratic Senator Mark Pryor trailed the Tea Party favorite, Tom Cotton, by 221,300 Facebook fans. Cotton won by 145,000 votes. In Kentucky, Democratic challenger Allison Grimes trailed Republican Minority Leader Mitch McConnell by 54,000 Facebook fans. McConnell won by 222,000 votes.

Republicans made a strategic choice to develop their messaging infrastructure using Facebook. Across the 11 most competitive senate races, they built up a two-to-one advantage in fans—682,000 to 330,000. Democrats beat them on engagement—152,000 to 93,000 per week. But the Republicans won all 11 of those races and that meant the losing Democratic candidates' Facebook fans and their engagement levels vanished, virtually overnight.

For the GOP victors, those 2 million Facebook fans became part of the party's messaging infrastructure. And because they had had such success with Facebook, Republicans and their Tea Party allies kept buying fans (or likes)—advertising to specific groups and demographics to increase their advantage in this new battle space. Their engagement levels grew over time as their social media gurus experimented with memes and videos. Three groups in particular led the way forward. ForAmerica, the National Rifle Association and FreedomWorks expanded to 18 million fans by the 2016 presidential election!

Unfortunately, Democratic strategists took a dim view of Facebook. They much preferred to spend their nearly unlimited resources the old fashioned way—buying television ads that vanished from voters' consciousness as soon as the buy ended. At the end of a campaign, all they were left with were snowflakes in a blizzard of commercial advertisements. Their experience in getting trounced by the GOP via Facebook was not an object lesson in campaign strategy that suggested a new approach. Instead it became viewed as a useless tool—so they gave up trying to master the new technology. It brought to mind a line by Strother Martin in the movie "Cool Hand Luke," "What we have here, is a failure to communicate!" And it became even more rusted from disuse.

The Republicans, by contrast, had a multi-layer infrastructure in place after their 2014 successes. They had incumbent congressmen, senators, governors and state legislators who, with proper training and message discipline, would hammer away at President Obama and the Democrats on a daily basis. They also had an incredible messaging platform, one that relied on their partisans to like and share the GOP content about Benghazi and Obamacare with their friends and family members, an infrastructure that enabled them to reach tens of millions of like-minded Americans each week.

The GOP's strategists had two more years to build and expand on that multi-layer infrastructure. They and their eventual presidential nominee would use it to devastating effect.

CHAPTER 29

LEVERAGING OUR VOTES

I am not unemployed because of the economy. The jobs are there, but I'm not in a field that is very typical for black women ... when people call me for interviews, they backpedal as soon as they hear my voice over the phone. I speak perfect English, but there is a distinct ethnicity in my voice, as there would be with anyone of any ethnicity. So when the name, my resume, or my zip code doesn't give me away, the voice usually does. They cut the conversation short as soon as I answer the phone ...

Edna's Unemployment Story

As 2015 dawned, the Union of Unemployed decided that its sole focus for the next two years was to retain Democratic control of the White House. It had to make the case that Democratic presidents from Franklin Delano Roosevelt to Barack Obama had used their power to lift up large segments of the population.

Roosevelt did so for the destitute of the Great Depression. Truman did it for the troops returning from World War II—desegregating the armed forces and pushing a Full Employment Bill. Kennedy literally opened the doors of higher education to African Americans in the south and, often too cautiously, encouraged the

Civil Rights Movement. Johnson, with his Great Society initiatives, reduced poverty for millions, particularly America's elderly. Carter created the Department of Education and began a decades-long effort to improve inner city schools. Clinton, while moving us toward a budget surplus, stimulated the economy and generated unprecedented levels of job growth. President Obama, while dealing with the worst financial crisis in seven decades, provided health insurance for 18 million uninsured Americans.

John F. Kennedy quoting Archimedes had said, "Give me a place where I can stand—and I shall move the world." In their own way, each of those Democratic presidents had done so. They were the indispensable force using the levers of government to move the world. In each case, it was the White House, not the Senate, the House of Representatives or the supreme court that led the way.

President Kennedy's quote was displayed with a photograph of the North Portico of the White House as the cover photo for the newly launched website page UCubed2016.org. Its tag line was "leveraging our votes" and was meant to instill confidence in the unemployed, underemployed and uncounted who visited the site. But the message was not simply cosmetic nor was it meant to be inspirational. It was part of a multi-year strategy, one driven by the realities of the Electoral College, one focused on the implicit power of the four early voting states to dictate who the next Democratic nominee would be, one dependent on, hopefully, engaging more than 600,000 Facebook activists in the final weeks of the 2016 presidential election.

The raison d'etre for UCubed had never changed: to help our Facebook activists and family members find jobs to match their skills, fair wages to feed their families, a shot at the dream and leaders who gave a damn. Sitting on the sidelines was not an option, neither was letting others emasculate the current president of the United States or permit others to pick the next occupant of the White House without a fight.

UCubed needed to grow from 250,000 to 600,000 Facebook fans. To be ultimately successful, it had to be an integral part of the next president's electoral coalition. After the victory was won, UCubed expected to be part of his or her governing coalition. Only then could UCubed have the most direct impact on the lives of the unemployed.

Our strategy all along was not aimed at winning one job for one individual. UCubed wanted to win 21 million jobs for those who had waited so long to resume their careers and restore the economic wellbeing of their families.

There was, however, a fatal flaw in the strategy: money.

There was also a catch-22. If you weren't invited to the Mandarin Hotel to pitch your strategy, capabilities and achievements, major Democratic donors ignored you. And their millions flowed freely but to fund a very different strategy.

Meeting just two weeks after the 2014 disaster, the *mandarins of money* had issued a new six year plan called Vision 2020 that doubled down on the same issues, demographics and tactics that had already cost the Democrats so dearly. It added single women to the litany of the rising American electorate and then took aim at the gubernatorial and state legislative races leading up to redistricting after the 2020 elections.

The *mandarins* (so nicknamed because of the hotel where they met) had spent more than $120 million in the 2014 cycle. Their millions, however, did not go to candidates but instead filled the coffers of Democratic consultants eager to produce thousands of television ads, direct mail pieces, automatic phone calls and deploy paid foot canvassers. Very few of those millions were used in the Facebook battle space.

Nor did the *mandarins'* money go to talk about the top issues—jobs and the economy—that motivated the working class to go vote. Quite frankly, the *mandarins* and their consultants couldn't find the working class with a divining rod and a GPS system. And yet, the white/no-college and non-white/no-college vote constituted 50 percent of the voter turnout in 2014.

As I argued in a vituperative Facebook post, the *mandarins of money* could not expect to diss half the electorate cycle after cycle and still expect to win. They could not consciously ignore working class issues—jobs that match their skills and fair wages to feed their families—because it might nick a few basis points off their own investments.

But they did.

The *mandarins of money* would continue to do so. And their millions would act as a magnet for candidates trying to navigate the uncharted waters of 2016 one year ahead of the first-in-the-nation caucuses in Iowa and primaries in New Hampshire.

So, in early January 2015, I e-mailed Dan Schwerin and others, once again, to press the case for working class Democrats. My memo started with "HRC now faces two improbable candidates—Bernie Sanders and Jim Webb. Alone they are not threats. In tandem, they are." It went on to explain:

> "Webb's only play comes in the rolling regional southern primary. But to be a credible alternative he needs to place second in NH or IA and win SC …
>
> By running to her left and aiming at college graduates, [Sanders] follows the path first blazed by Gary Hart and later by Barack Obama. Bernie Sanders is not a working class champion but

a candidate that appeals to the progressive elites. And, just as Elizabeth Warren would do, Sanders would force HRC into a contest with Webb for roughly half the Democratic electorate.

Sanders is no fool. He has a Facebook page with nearly a million likes [or fans]. His politics aside, his sound bites are designed to appeal to those progressives and liberals who feel burned by Obama. Iowa is the perfect state to play on that disenchantment albeit with a national audience watching. Its pacifism, progressive politics and farm communities are a close match for Sanders' Vermont voters."

While Webb would drop out before Iowa's caucuses, Sanders would find Iowa an almost perfect match for his politics.

The memo then turned to working class Democrats in Iowa and New Hampshire. It suggested that they could be a dominant political force in both states. And it reviewed how non-college and college educated voters drove the results in the Clinton–Obama contests eight years earlier:

"In the 40 largest school districts covering two-thirds of [New Hampshire's] population, Obama won six out of nine school districts where 33.3% or more of the population had college degrees. HRC won two districts: Nashua and Merrimack. Bedford was a tie. In school districts with between 29% and 33.2% of college graduates, HRC won six out of eight. And below 28.9%, she swept the remaining 23 districts...

In Iowa, those with college degrees comprised more than 30 percent of the population in just 35 of its 354 school districts. Those 35 school districts contain only one-fifth of the state's population. Not surprisingly, three-fifths of those elite school districts are found in six counties—Polk, Story, Dallas, Johnson, Scott and Linn. And those school districts are not countywide. But they do influence the politics of their counties.

In the 2008 caucuses, those 35 elite districts could be found in 21 counties. Obama won 26.8% of his statewide tally of delegates in those counties. Clinton won 19.1% of hers."

The math and mapping wasn't as precise as I would have liked. But the facts spoke for themselves. Those with college degrees were a distinct minority in Iowa and New Hampshire. More than that, you could predict political outcomes based on their concentration in a school district. More than 30 percent meant middle and upper middle class voters; less than 30 percent meant working and lower class voters. As the percentage of college degree holders dropped even further below the 30 percent mark, the greater percentage of votes were cast for Hillary Clinton. The reverse was also true. As the percentage of college degree holders increased above the 30 percent mark, the greater percentage of votes were cast for Barack Obama.

The voters with college degrees were geographically concentrated in far fewer and far more elite schools districts. In the past, they had turned out in greater numbers than working class Democrats had. They were more responsive to appeals from candidates like Gary Hart, Michael Dukakis, Paul Tsongas, Bill Bradley, John Kerry and Barack Obama.

And yet, most of the candidates who targeted the working class— Walter Mondale, Bill Clinton and Al Gore, for example—prevailed over the long haul. Had they been able to turn out working class Democrats in Iowa and/or New Hampshire their races would have ended, successfully, by the Ides of March.

Even as I hit the *send* button, I sensed that I was losing the argument within the nascent Clinton campaign. So, anxiously, I fired off another e-mail in late February to Sherwin and added Lissa Muscatine, a family friend and Hillary's former speechwriter at the Department of State, to the recipients. The subject line read, "Who, What, Why":

"This week, as you gather to craft HRC's message, look around the room. Ask yourself which person is offering insights into the 146.8 million working class Americans, the 22.3 million unemployed and unemployed and the 12 million plus union members. If the answer is no one, then one of the most basic questions—WHO is our audience—was left off the agenda. And a campaign cannot craft a message without a clear sense of its intended audience(s).

Nor should a message drive strategy. A complete strategy lays out WHAT must be done to (a) win the nomination—2,242+ delegates, (b) the electoral College—270+ Electoral Votes and (c) successfully govern for eight years—engaging 65 million Hillary voters on an ongoing basis.

Message's most important role, however, is defining WHY is Hillary running. Part of the answer is deeply personal and can only come from her. But a larger part of the answer comes from the challenges she will face as president. Are there existential threats to our way of life? Is it ISIL and terrorism? Is it wage stagnation and inequality? Is it the power of money to purchase results in Congress, not just access? Or is it our growing inability to govern ourselves?"

Previously and based on my experience on Facebook, I had suggested to the three of them that our 238-year experiment in self-government was foundering. The winds of change had driven us off our intended course. The forces of extremism were battering us from all sides. And perilous obstacles lay in our path.

In what was described as an imaginary announcement speech, I argued that, under our constitution, the people possessed the power and the president acted on their behalf. Whatever power he, or preferably she, exercised came directly from them. Whatever she did or did not do was done in their name. She was their agent; they were her employer.

Oddly, somewhere along the way, Americans had forgotten how crucial, how absolutely vital their role was. We forgot that it wasn't public opinion polls that sampled only a portion of the population that held the power; the people did. We forgot that it wasn't the media or the corporations that held the power; the people did. We forgot that that power—our power, our power as free men and women, our power as citizens of this great country—was what the president relied on to get things done in our name.

No one person, not JFK or certainly not Archimedes even with a longer lever, could move the world. The presidency was not—and never has been—a job for one man or one woman. It was a job that relied on the talents, dedication and sacrifice of us all.

In our representative democracy, the presidency was the only institution that was elected by *all* the people. And their responsibility did not end when the ballots were counted. Their responsibility continued on for four long years whether or not their "guy" won or their "gal" did.

We, the *people* had a role to play every day and not just on election day. We were advocates and opponents on specific policies or programs. But we were not permanent and implacable foes. We were all Americans, first and foremost. We came from different time zones, different parties, different religious traditions, different national, racial and ethnic backgrounds, different sexual preferences. But we came together to forge our nation's future.

We had an obligation, a sacred obligation, to prove to the world that our *experiment in democracy* produced peace and prosperity, formed a more perfect union, insured justice for all. To us, those ideals weren't throwaway lines. That was who we were as Americans. And that was what free people did.

It was our job to govern ourselves. It was also our job to pass along that all-too-precious and remarkable gift of self-government on to the next generation.

And then along came Donald Trump.

CHAPTER 30

WORKING CLASS DEMOCRATS

My family and friends are not in a position to help, even though they try desperately. I am not the only long term unemployed in my family. Our steel town has been devastated by this recession. I just don't know what else we can do. We cannot afford to live anymore.

Shay's Unemployment Story

On April 12, 2015, via a YouTube video, Hillary Clinton announced that she was running for president. "Everyday Americans need a champion," she said directly to the camera. "And I want to be that champion."

The following day, during her formal presidential campaign announcement on Roosevelt Island, Hillary Clinton spoke about working class Americans. Early in her speech, she explained that she was "running to make our economy work for you and for every American."[30] Her riff continued:

"For the successful and the struggling.

For the innovators and inventors.

For those breaking barriers in technology and discovering cures for diseases.

For the factory workers and food servers who stand on their feet all day.

For the nurses who work the night shift.

For the truckers who drive for hours and the farmers who feed us.

For the veterans who served our country.

For the small business owners who took a risk.

For everyone who's ever been knocked down, but refused to be knocked out."

Later she referenced her "invisibles" by saying, "I had the honor of representing brave firefighters, police officers, EMTs, construction workers, and volunteers who ran toward danger on 9/11 and stayed there, becoming sick themselves."

Then, a few paragraphs later, Hillary talked about "a single mom juggling a job and classes at community college, while raising three kids. She doesn't expect anything to come easy. But she did ask me: What more can be done so it isn't quite so hard for families like hers?"

"I want to be her champion and your champion" was the next line in Secretary Clinton's announcement speech. It was the exactly right answer to the woman's question. It reprised the best line of her YouTube video. And it also answered the plea I made in an open letter to Hillary Clinton and posted two weeks earlier on UCubed.

Had the speech stopped there, I might have died a happy man.

Her announcement speech continued on and on and on detailing every policy and stroking every constituency of the Democratic Party. It lasted 46 minutes—shorter than most State of the Union Speeches but containing almost as many policy initiatives. Taken in its totality, the speech signaled that sooner rather than later "Hillary for America" would need a more thematic speech, one that focused entirely on working class Democrats.

I could not be the one either to write or critique such a speech. Knowing that UCubed would endorse Hillary Clinton after polling its Facebook activists and that it would then try to make good on its endorsement, I had cut myself off from contact with the Clinton campaign staff weeks before. Neither I nor any Union of Unemployed board members, staff or consultants could coordinate our efforts with the campaign. Federal law was explicit on that point. So for the next nine months, I remained the ultimate outsider to a campaign and candidate I desperately wanted to succeed.

The Survey Monkey polling of UCubed members took place over the next few weeks. The outcome was almost preordained. Hillary Clinton had outpaced her prospective challengers in the Democratic Party in two earlier polls. And she clobbered Bernie Sanders when the endorsement question was posed. Three-fifths of the respondents said UCubed should endorse Hillary Clinton for president of the United States.

We did.

The Union of Unemployed also embarked almost immediately on its Working Class Democrats Project. Originally, it was intended to lead up to a Labor Day message from Tom Buffenbarger and Leo Hindery, Jr., and a draft stump speech for general use in early October—both would be based upon polling done by a well-known and reputable firm. And there would be an as-yet ill-defined Facebook campaign aimed at working class Democrats in the four early voting states of Iowa, New Hampshire, South Carolina and Nevada plus the band of southern states that would be voting on March 1, 2016.

Mark Mellman of the Mellman Group won the contract to poll working class Democrats; Tom Bonier of TargetSmart was commissioned to do the modeling of working class voters in the four early states. Both men were superb analysts and leaders in their respective fields. And yet, without Leo Hindery's substantial support, the project would have been stillborn.

I asked Mellman to explore how UCubed could motivate working class Democrats to vote for Hillary Clinton in the states that would be voting before March 1. For purposes of the survey, "working class" was defined as having less than a college degree. There were several assumptions I wanted the poll to test:

> "For working class Democrats—white, black and Latino—the last seven years [have] meant severe economic hardships. Lost jobs, lost incomes, lost assets and lost opportunities have denied them a fair shot at the American Dream. Even when they found a job, they faced much lower pay scales, stagnating wages, little overtime and stealthily higher costs for necessities. They've become more cynical about government, more cautious about their personal spending, and less trusting of both corporate and political leaders.

> So, motivating them to attend the caucuses or vote in primaries may be difficult. The anger and alienation they once felt has turned to icy indifference. And while they were excited and even enervated by Hillary Clinton and Barack Obama in 2008, they feel burned out and see little reason to go vote eight years later. In fact, they feel abandoned by the Democratic Party which to them seems more intent on protecting the upper middle class, the rising American electorate—whatever that is—and the millionaires and billionaires who fund their campaigns.

The problem, as they see it, is that Democratic politicians say they're for the little guy but only truly care about their own careers. So, when push comes to shove, working class Democrats get the short end of the stick. Just look at our dilapidated schools, our torn up streets and clogged highways, our closed factories and stores, our nearly empty wallets—and the Democrats haven't done squat. So WTF. Why go out of our way to vote for them? We're completely invisible to them.

If the key test for working class Democrats is 'does s/he care about folks like me' and not a string of issue positions, then motivating these marginalized voters isn't accomplished by word-smithing more nuanced policies or splitting hairs over programs. They have to FEEL that a candidate gives a damn about them. And so do their friends and family members. And that means speaking directly about their lives and connecting with them at a gut level, not with a plethora of words but with simple acts of a trusted friend."

Testing those assumptions would give us a better handle on how to communicate with those working class Democrats. But I also needed to know what messages might motivate them to go to a caucus or vote in a primary.

So I asked Mellman to test whether or not specific messages about jobs, skills and prices might resonate with working class Democrats. Did they echo what they were thinking? Did they provide a way to connect with them at a gut level? The Mellman Group conducted the survey in early August 2015. And its results stunned even an experienced pollster like Mark Mellman. His key findings were as follows:

Working-Class Democrats see themselves treading water financially and worry about jobs and income inequality.

A significant majority believe Democrats care, but some question their willingness to fight for policies that will benefit the working class...

Clinton has a large lead among non-college Democrats, and elicits strong enthusiasm (emphasis added)...

The caucus states those who ID as downscale and those with no college attendance are among the most abundant targets for mobilization.

The entire poll was quickly published on the UCubed website and linked to posts on Facebook. Those steps enabled me to widely share its data with other labor leaders, political leaders, and individuals and organizations involved in the 2016 presidential campaign.

It also led to another open letter to Hillary Clinton. This one was also posted to the UCubed Facebook page. It explained that "working class Democrats were asked about three of their party's top priorities—raising the minimum wage, paid sick leave and equal pay for women. One-fifth said the policies wouldn't help them in a meaningful way. One-third said they might help but Democrats wouldn't fight hard enough to enact them." It continued:

> "Deeply cynical or just being realistic? Either way, the connection between working class Democrats and their leaders has frayed to a dangerous and potentially irreparable point.

> So the UCubed survey tested messages that might resonate with working class Democrats. Two messages that three-quarters of the respondents said would make them 'somewhat enthusiastic' or 'very enthusiastic' about a presidential candidate echoed what you've been saying:

> MESSAGE A: The last seven years have meant severe economic hardships for many of us. Lost jobs, lost assets and lost opportunities have denied us a fair shot at the American Dream. Jobs are still scarce, and jobs where we can earn a fair

wage, feed our families and pay the bills are even harder to find. And yet, politicians in Washington don't seem to care. It's time to stop acting like working Americans are invisible.

MESSAGE B: Too many politicians say they're for the little guy but only truly care about their own careers. So, when push comes to shove, working Americans get the short end of the stick. Just look at our dilapidated schools, our torn-up streets and clogged highways, our closed factories, our nearly empty wallets—and no one in Washington is doing anything about it. It's time to fight for the rights and opportunities of working Americans, not just those at the top."

Other possible messages drew slightly higher enthusiasm scores. They were short, action-oriented statements about affordable child care, putting people to work and leveling the playing field. They struck a nerve but only briefly.

"How do you convince working class Democrats who are so disengaged from, and disgusted by, politics to go vote or attend a caucus? How do you turn deeply embedded apathy and indifference into genuine excitement and enthusiasm?

It's pretty simple. Talk to them. Directly.

Working class Democrats are waiting to hear your clarion call to action once again. They want YOU to be THEIR champion."

By the time this missive was posted, however, the Clinton campaign had moved on from its earlier theme of "Everyday Americans need a champion. I want to be that champion." And her "invisibles" were growing even more invisible, if that was even possible, with each passing day.

The Mellman survey was used by Tom Bonior and the folks at TargetSmart to inform their modeling process. They did a second survey of 6,000 working class Democrats. Their modeling then generated a list of

386,000 non-college Democrats who were registered to vote, would support Hillary Clinton in a general election, but were unlikely to attend a caucus or vote in a primary.

In a complete departure from prior campaigns, Tom Bonior worked with Experian, the credit score giant, to create a subcategory of Facebook users. Experian ran its Facebook user data against TargetSmart's 386,000 working class Democrats and matched 90,000 records! It was a eureka moment for UCubed. Our nearly 375,000 Facebook activists had 90,000 brothers and sisters in those all-so-critical early states.

This cutting-edge technology had been used only once before and that was in a statewide issue campaign in Texas. UCubed could now message working class Democrats—12,000 in Iowa, 36,500 in New Hampshire, 21,000 in Nevada and 20,700 in South Carolina—directly and repeatedly.

UCubed with its 378,000 Facebook activists spanned the entire country. By boosting our memes and posts and videos—paying Facebook to expand our audience—we could reach hundreds of thousands of their friends and family members in the 13 states voting on March 1, 2016.

All UCubed needed now was for the creative juices to flow in order to find a way to turn Mellman's messaging results and Bonior's modeling into a powerhouse campaign to turn out working class Democrats, registered voters who were overwhelmingly supportive of Hillary Clinton but were also unlikely to attend a caucus or go to the polls.

CHAPTER 31

BLINKING LIGHTS

Thank you for your compassion! Too many people judge us unemployed folks, think we're just lazy and just sitting around sucking up the "grand" benefits of unemployment dough. Yeah right. I'm on the verge of losing my home and living out of my vehicle ... I hope I'm still around to see the recovery in our economy. I just don't know how to make it anymore. I am all tapped out.

Financially and mentally ... just need a job, any job will do!

Susan's Unemployment Story

Before the long Labor Day weekend, Tom Buffenbarger and Leo Hindery published "What do Working Class Democrats Want?" in the *Huffington Post*. Its powerful message was seen by thousands of union members and hundreds of labor leaders as they prepared to celebrate a three-day weekend first suggested by a Machinists leader.

The title of their piece built upon Samuel Gompers' famous quote: "What does labor want? We want more schoolhouses and less jails; more books and less arsenals; more learning and less vice; more leisure and less greed; more justice and less revenge; in fact, more of the opportunities to cultivate our better natures, to make manhood more noble, womanhood more beautiful, and childhood more happy and bright."

Gompers was the first and longest-serving president of the American Federation of Labor. His quote came from an 1893 speech he delivered in Chicago. Now Tom Buffenbarger, the longest-serving president of the Machinists, would be retiring in just four months. That fact would have enormous yet unforeseen consequences for the Union of Unemployed and, by extension, Hillary Clinton's campaign for president.

Buffenbarger and Hindery's op-ed used the data from the Mellman poll, particularly its finding that only 31 percent of non-college Democrats thought that their children would be better off than they were. "In other words," they wrote, "for seven out of ten working class Democrats, the promise of the American Dream, around which they've based their lives, has instead become a mirage." After discussing the survey's other findings, Buffenbarger and Hindery concluded:

> "And while we tested their preferences for president and the likelihood of their voting in a primary or attending a caucus, this is not the time to explore Hillary Clinton's 5 to 1 advantage over her closest competitor. Besides, those numbers will change—and hopefully grow—as campaigns focus more closely on this massive subset of voters who could decide the Democratic Party's nominee by March 1, 2016.
>
> We say 'hopefully' because working class Democrats are seldom targeted by presidential campaigns intent on micro-targeting tiny slivers of the electorate. They're not the late-breaking undecideds, not the readily persuadable, not the ones motivated by a single issue and not easily turned on or turned out. They're good people with strong opinions for whom politics has become a spectator sport.

On this Labor Day, presidential candidates will tweet their paeans to working Americans. Few will talk about the unemployed, underemployed and uncounted whose numbers have grown the working class over the last seven years. Fewer still, if any, will spend Labor Day kicking back and playing with the kids and grandchildren of working class Democrats.

And that's a damn shame. If they did, they would learn what working class Democrats care about most—making certain their kids and grandchildren will be better off than they are— and from that one insight they might construct a campaign for the presidency that will resonate with working class Americans of every political persuasion."

Not surprisingly, no presidential candidate of either party took them up on the challenge inherent in the call to kick back and play with those kids and grandchildren. But UCubed, even as early as Labor Day weekend, was testing ads that focused directly on that age cohort.

On September 3, UCubed posted a photo of an infant covered with a pink blanket and staring intently into the distance. The upper caption read, "Voting? Hmmm. I would if I could." The lower caption read, "But I can't. I gotta rely on you to go vote … and then make my life better." It was designed to reach the 69 percent of working class Democrats who believed their kids would *not* be better off than their parents.

Facebook reported that our pink blanket baby post drew 7,000 likes, comments and shares. It reached 98,000 people. And with those data points, Glenn Totten and I started designing a Facebook-centric campaign that for once would *not* use animated cartoons but instead would introduce potential voters to a series of crying babies.

By the fall of 2015, UCubed had grown to 343,000 Facebook fans whose friends and family members numbered almost 3.5 million. Those numbers would only grow as it continued to invest its limited resources in Facebook ads that generated new *likes* or fans for the UCubed pages.

And money—to buy likes, develop the crying baby concept, pay for Facebook ads aimed at working class Democrats and meet overhead obligations including salaries—was in short supply. The Machinists' monthly contribution of $20,000 was carefully hoarded to provide a buffer in uncertain times. Leo Hindery's contributions funded the Mellman poll and the TargetSmart modeling. And, thankfully, Leo was willing to help us fundraise.

At the same time, "Hillary for America" was also soliciting donors. I was invited to hear Jake Sullivan, Clinton's policy guru, speak to a small group in Washington. I leapt at the chance.

As I listened to his presentation and the questions and answers that followed, I knew that working class Democrats couldn't care less about the nuanced, extremely thoughtful and well-researched policies Sullivan was describing. They only wanted to know if Hillary gave a damn about them and their families.

Hillary's theme about being their champion was a distant memory. In its place were a string of issues that blinked on and off like Christmas lights—now you see them, now you don't. As bright as they shone for a few seconds, the linkages between those bursts of brilliance were invisible. To the guy working a drill press, the gal scanning groceries or the kids searching for a job, there were no visible linkages. In a Facebook post the following day, I tried to explain what was missing:

"What's missing or, more accurately, what cannot be seen is the wiring for, and the electricity to power, those lights. The wiring is the narrative that connects those individual lights—it's the WHY she runs and the WHY she cares so deeply.

The unseeable electricity is the WHAT that drives Hillary to get up again every time she gets knocked down. The WHAT is the energy she draws from the people she meets and the folks she knows are counting on her.

And hundreds of thousands are."

Given the ban on coordination, I never spoke with nor asked a question of Jake Sullivan. His mastery of both foreign and domestic issues was impressive. But what he did not know was that working class Democrats wanted to hear the *why* and see the *what* before committing to going the extra miles to a caucus or polling booth for Hillary Clinton. So the post continued:

> "To turn them on and, more importantly, to turn them out for the caucuses and primaries in February, Jake Sullivan and the crew in the Brooklyn campaign office had to realize that the electricity—the WHAT—is not generated by the candidate or her campaign. The electricity comes from that vast pool of potential voters and caucus goers who decide they really, really do like Hillary.
>
> Until the wiring—the narrative of WHY she runs and WHY she cares so deeply—is illuminated for them to see, the blinking lights are just a series of unconnected issues. And working class Democrats don't 'do' issues. They don't 'do' nuances. They 'do' gut checks. Then they 'do' the she-gets-it test. And, eventually, they 'do' their she-gives-a-damn exam."

More than a bit of irony attaches to that post. Its metaphor of blinking lights and electricity was meant to deliver a low wattage jolt to a campaign that had no intention of focusing on white working class Democrats. Instead it was relying on the "rising American electorate" to deliver victories in the caucuses and primaries that lay ahead.

What I did not know was how soon the plug would be pulled on the Union of Unemployed. Our electricity was to be cut off abruptly.

CHAPTER 32

CRYING DIAPER BABIES

I am a 43-year-old unemployed father now a stay-at-home dad. My position as a shipping and receiving manager was eliminated due to company downsizing March 5th of 2008. I have exhausted all my unemployment benefits ... my wife has to work overtime so that we can get by. I have to watch our 20-month-old daughter as we cannot afford child care. I have been looking for work every day since I was shut out of my job but no one will hire me.

Michael's Unemployment Story

In the first weeks of December 2015, two numbers changed ever so slightly. The BLS' *official* unemployment rate dropped below 5 percent. The Federal Reserve raised its benchmark interest rate by 25/100th of a point, signaling the end of their stimulus efforts. With clinking champagne glasses, pundits, politicians and investors celebrated their versions of full-employment.

America's jobless did not.

Leo Hindery's monthly summary put real unemployed persons at 15.9 million and then added 4.1 million who wanted to work but hadn't looked in the last year. His bottom line calculation was 20 million people were unemployed and the *real* unemployment rate was 12 percent.

There were, however, three other numbers to celebrate: 359,957 . . . 806,468 . . . 10,788,078. They were the number of UCubed fans, its engaged users and their total reach, respectively, in a single seven-day period!

UCubed, conceptually, began as a math problem. How could *you* be *cubed—you* raised to the third power—in order to build your own political power?

Never in a million years had I imagined that a six-sided cube could reach the ninth power. But it did. If you multiply six by itself *nine* times, you get 10,077,696—or about 711,000 fewer people than UCubed's total reach that first week in December 2015.

We, as a people, had come a long way in the past seven years. Way back in August 2009, there were more than 30.6 million Americans who were unemployed, underemployed or uncounted. Real unemployment now sat at 20 million. UCubed never claimed to have "saved" or "created" a single one of those 11 million jobs. That wasn't our core mission.

Ending the isolation the jobless endured was. So we had tried to get the unemployed, underemployed and uncounted to communicate with each other, to reach out to their friends and family members. That was why our original website enabled folks to create a cube and build neighborhoods. And it was why we shifted to become a Facebook-centric nonprofit.

Explaining, enraging, engaging, entertaining and empowering the jobless were also part of our core mission. From generating 60,000 e-mails to the Congress in 2010 to running our BEE MAD @ THE GOP and Chamo the Chameleon campaigns in 2012 and 2014, we enabled the unemployed to become a virtual political army delivering, literally, tens of millions of messages to their friends and family members each election cycle.

What UCubed and its 378,000 fans accomplished was unique in the annals of American politics. It turned the powerless into a potent force for change. It ended the isolation the unemployed had endured silently in past recessions. And it enabled them to fight for jobs that matched their skills, fair wages to feed their families, an even shot at the dream and leaders who gave a damn.

As 2015 came to a close, UCubed tallied up what it had accomplished in a single year. Its posts had engaged 15.6 million fans, friends, and family members; its total reach had exceeded 218 million Facebook users!

Not too shabby.

Before Christmas, UCubed tested its first Crying Diaper Baby meme in Iowa and New Hampshire. A photo of a baby with an angry scowl making him look like Winston Churchill minus the cigar carried the caption "Great schools and great teachers aren't a dime a dozen. Go vote for Me!" Or, in the case of Iowa, "Go caucus for ME!" The meme targeted the personal Facebook pages of 48,400 working class Democrats in those two states. The test demonstrated that the meme reached 31,669 of the targeted audience and engaged 800 of them at a cost of $992—or *three cents* per person reached.

To the miser in me, that was a huge advantage. Sending a single piece of direct mail to those 48,400 working class Democrats would have cost upwards of $30,000 and their only engagement would be tossing the mailer in the trash. In this first test, 800 recipients liked, shared or commented on the meme and took it viral to 160,000 friends and family members.

Before the New Year, those working class Democrats in Iowa and New Hampshire saw the Angry Baby meme three more times and Crying Baby Girl meme twice. That second meme pictured a little girl with tears streaming down her face and the caption "Grandpa built a better life for his kids. So can you!" And each meme carried the tag line "GO vote (or caucus) for ME!" appropriate to its targeted state. Total daily reach climbed over the 100,000 mark and engagement grew to 2,000.

On January 5, our first Baby Talk video hit our target audience's Facebook pages. Created by Totten Communications, it featured actual human beings instead of our usual animated characters and the kids weren't infants in diapers. They were slightly older, talked on cellphones just like adults did and delivered a potent message:

"What are those guys doing?

They're cutting education that's what they're doing.

So how are we going to get good jobs?

Our future is going to be murder.

And we can't do anything.

But you can.

Come on, get off your butt.

Go vote. You're all we've got."

Baby Talk reached 7,200 in Iowa or 60 percent of our target audience. In New Hampshire, it reached 15,400 or 42 percent of our targeted working class Democrats. But the amazing and exciting thing was that 11,000 folks who saw the video in the two states liked, shared or commented on the video. In short, Baby Talk went viral.

Two days later, the same thing happened. Baby Talk reached 7,800 in Iowa, 15,300 in New Hampshire and engaged 12,300 across the two states. And, when it ran in South Carolina and Nevada on January 14 and 16, this GOTV message to working class Democrats reached 14,800 in the Palmetto State and 15,300 in the Silver State. It engaged another 5,400 Facebook users with those two posts.

And then, our plug was pulled.

Before Tom Buffenbarger retired, the IAM Executive Council voted unanimously to fund the Union of Unemployed for 2016. Their $20,000 per month commitment was our major funding source and its first install-ment had been electronically deposited in the UCubed bank account. But the new executive council led by Bobby Martinez met and unanimously rescinded its annual commitment knowing full well that that would put UCubed out of business. And it did.

Slowly.

Painfully.

Martinez had not been the first choice to succeed Buffenbarger, not even the second. He was a distant third choice, a choice that several on the executive council who eyed the IAM jet and the other perks of the international president's office made expecting that Martinez would be a "short-termer." Yet Martinez thought he could count on his colleagues undying loyalty.

Fat chance.

The Machinists and Hillary for America would pay an enormous and enduring price for Martinez's own disloyalty—to his mentor, Tom Buffenbarger, and to his union's highest profile member, Hillary Clinton.[31] For loyalty is a two-way street. And once the signs are changed overnight to one-way, there is always the chance of a debilitating, head-on accident or two.

Still, with what money was left in the bank, a round of fundraising calls and a personal donation to my favorite nonprofit, I was able to keep the Crying Diaper Baby campaign alive. Barely. Leo Hindery was extremely generous. But the unions that contributed in the past or promised to con-tribute in 2016 shied away. So did *friends* who assumed the worst.

Six more memes and one more video landed in the Facebook pages of those 90,000 working class Democrats in the four early voting states. They were also boosted—by investing up to $1,500 per post—to UCubed Facebook activists, their family members and their friends nationwide.

The Crying Diaper Baby memes kept hammering away at the messaging developed from Mark Mellman's poll. And their off-beat humor juxtaposed against close-ups of crying infants seemed to work:

"Wanna see a growth spurt. I'd invest in schools, roads and research labs.

Do a sniff test. If GOP tax cuts smell like a diaper, expect the worst.

Anchor baby? No way. I'm proud to be an All-American.

My folks need a raise. These cheap-o diapers leak like a sieve.

Today we depend on you ... but tomorrow you'll depend on us.

Afraid of terrorists? I'm scared you won't go vote/caucus. Take me along."

Those pictures of crying babies with the tag line of "Go Vote For ME!" kept racking up huge numbers in the four early voting states.

In between "my folks need a raise" and "today we depend on you" we slotted in a second GOTV video. Called Baby Dialogue, it used most of the same kids from the earlier video and added a few more for their sound effects. Its dialogue, again using cellphones like their parents did, went like this:

"Did you hear this?

They're talking about putting anchors on babies.

What? Like our student loans won't be enough to drag us under.

What are we going to do?

We've gotta get everyone to vote.

Mom … Dad … Nana … Pops …

How are we going to get them all to the polls?

Volume!

(10 seconds of babies crying at the top of the lungs)

I like it.

It's simple. No vote, no sleep.

Come on, let's go vote."

And it worked. On two levels.

The Crying Baby memes and videos reached 667,000 working class Democrats—non-college, unlikely voters or caucus goers—in the four early voting states. It engaged 72,000 of our modeled and targeted audience, which spread the message even further. We hit our Iowans ten times, our New Hampshire and South Carolina targets seven times and our Nevadans six times. By boosting those posts nationally, our total reach—paid and organic—grew to 3 million and we engaged nearly 800,000 Facebook users.

What mattered most was turnout. Did UCubed move enough of those working class Democrats who liked Hillary Clinton but were unlikely voters or caucus goers to "get off their butts" to make a difference? Sadly, UCubed didn't have the money left to prove that they did.

But this I do know: Hillary Clinton won Iowa by 400 caucus goers. She won Nevada by 4,400. And UCubed had repeated contacts with the unlikeliest of voters in those two states. We had given those 11,900 working class Democrats in Iowa and 21,000 working class Democrats in Nevada our best shot.

Secretary Clinton also won the South Carolina primary by 175,000 votes where, owing to a cash crunch, UCubed had cut back its Facebook-centric ads.

Equally important, UCubed was the only organization whose nation-wide messaging reached working class Democrats in the March 1 or Super Tuesday states. In the Alabama, Arkansas and Tennessee primaries eight years earlier, working class Democrats accounted for 61 percent to 65 percent of the Democratic turnout. In Texas, they were 58 percent. In Georgia and Virginia, they were 48 percent and 43 percent of the Democratic turnout, respectively. And Hillary Clinton would go on to win each of those states, primarily, by focusing on Black and Latino communities who were part and parcel of the working class Democrats UCubed sought to reach.

Someday, when the data files are updated to include the voters and caucus goers in those four early voting states, and, perhaps, even in those six southern states, we will know for certain whether or not those crying babies got Mom, Dad, Nana and Pops to the polls.

CHAPTER 33

A RED TEAM STRATEGY

I lost my job as a dispatcher for a trucking company when there was no freight to move. I have seen no changes in the economy here ... creditors have grown tired of hearing I have no money and quite frankly so have I ... I, too, am a very hard working taxpayer that has a very long memory and I will keep all this info for my choice at election time. Even if it means I am voting while I am living on the streets.

Carmen's Unemployment Story

As February ended and March began, the Union of Unemployed's board of directors met on phone. It decided to see if we could sell off or give away the only real assets the nonprofit had: the 350,000 fans on the UCubed Facebook page and the 28,000 Spanish language fans on its sister page Union De Desempleados. It also urged me to keep posting but cut spending unless and until new sources of revenue could be found.

It was wise advice.

Ultimately, the Spanish language page was transferred to Farmworker Justice, an organization led by Bruce Goldstien and renowned for its advocacy work on behalf of low wage farmhands, many of whom were immigrants. The much larger UCubed page was transferred to Tiller, a social media start-up located in San Francisco and led by David Feighan. Both transfers would take weeks, if not months, to complete and, in the interim, I kept posting about what was happening in the Republican and Democratic contests.

On February 25, I posted "An Insurmountable Lead" and projected that after Super Tuesday's primaries and caucuses the pledged delegate count would be 472 for Hillary Clinton and 299 for Bernie Sanders. That estimate did not count Clinton's overwhelming support among Super Delegates. If those were counted, Hillary would have 917 delegates and Bernie would have 317.

I argued that a 600-delegate lead was insurmountable based on the same matrix I had shown Mark Penn eight years earlier. Even though there were 42 jurisdictions (think states plus territories) still to vote, the writing was on the wall. Hillary Clinton would be the Democratic nominee.

Four days later, I posted "The Light Brigade," a short piece analyzing Donald Trump's 50 million interactions on Facebook and 6.1 million tweets mentioning him. He had crushed his opposition—Republicans and Democrats alike—on social media.

His 56.1 million interactions . . . in a week . . . nearly topped the 59.9 million votes John McCain received in the 2008 general election and the 60.9 million votes Mitt Romney ended up with four years later. Trump's army of 5.9 million Facebook fans and 6.4 million Twitter followers was engaged. They were sharing his posts and tweets with their friends and family—and those 56.1 million interactions per week rippled out to, literally, hundreds of millions of Facebook and Twitter users.

"Who needs MSNBC, CBS News or FOX News," I asked, "when Trump's cell phone can ignite a violent thunderstorm of lightning, hail and driving rain—nationwide? Why care about the *Washington Post* or *New*

York Times when you have 12.3 million Facebook and Twitter users willing to like or retweet you[r] message? Clearly, Trump doesn't."

All the television ads run by Jeb Bush, Ted Cruz and Marco Rubio were, at least to me, the equivalent of Tennyson's vivid description of the horses and riders in his poem *The Charge of the Light Brigade*, the classic example of bringing a knife to a gunfight. A quantum leap in political warfare was taking place, and just as cannon fire trumped cavalry sabers in the Valley of Death, social media trumped field organization and paid media in 2016. It was transforming not just campaign tactics but political strategy as well.

In late February, Tom Buffenbarger and I met with John Podesta, the Chairman of Hillary for America. Buffenbarger had asked for the meeting to make certain Podesta knew all that UCubed had done to support his candidate, including its messaging work with working class Democrats.

Podesta knew the campaign was turning into a slog, that the rural and suburban counties that Hillary had won in 2008 were becoming Sanders' territory, and that Sanders' hold on white working class Democrats was solidifying. My talking points from the meeting included the following:

"Recapture the sense that Hillary cares deeply about working families. Since last summer, her 'cares about people like me' has cratered from 65% in our Mellman poll to 17% in the New Hampshire exit poll. That 48 point drop is reversible.

Stop talking about issues and start talking about people's lives. Show she understands the problems of real people. 50% of working class Democrats feel they're falling behind. 69% say their kids won't live better lives. 68% say their finances haven't improved since the Great Recession.

Have her touch REAL people. Let them tell their story from where they live and work. Lose the stage, podium and events in a box. Take HRC into their homes, schools, factories, small businesses, churches, bars and recreation centers. Let her interact!

Attack Sanders['] strengths. His political revolution is dangerous, disingenuous, and ultimately destructive.

Revolutions appeal to intellectuals . . . the working class always pays the price.

Revolutions are a risky business, rely on the sly lie, and destroy lives. Just ask....

Revolutions tear apart communities and families, tear down what we've built together.

Use that line of attack to win back working class Democrats who are solid citizens and extremely patriotic.

Applaud their patriotism— their hard work built us up, their skills kept us moving, their sacrifices kept us strong. Acknowledge how hard it's been, how much they're hurting.

Explain how we're a Nation of Builders. And it's time to draw up new plans, invent new products and processes, reorganize and retrain our workforce, sharpen and invent new tools, and get back to building a new America and rebuilding our democratic institutions.

Focus on jobs and monthly bills. Contrast Sanders['] and Clinton's National Infrastructure Bank proposals to show how his pie-in-the-sky and her meat-and-potatoes approach impacts their job prospects.

His $1 trillion in taxes will be passed on to the working class, eventually. His promise of 13 million jobs is stillborn without a trillion dollars in new taxes—a tax increase that a GOP-controlled Congress will never approve. No tax increase. No bank. No jobs.

Her public-private partnership produces 3.9 million jobs with a one-time $25 billion appropriation. Investors—banks, pension funds, governments, corporations—provide financing on an 8 or 10 to one basis. The risk shifts to the billionaire class.

Offer them relief from debilitating pressure of stagnant wages and monthly bills. Sanders' obsession with Wall Street obscures how the Koch Brothers use so-called independent [regulatory] agencies to ratchet up consumer costs.

Captive agencies raise electricity and natural gas rates; cell phone, internet and cable tv fees; and interest rates on home mortgages, student and auto loans and credit cards balances.

In GOP-controlled states, captive agency rate-making demands a watch dog role for, if not aggressive intervention by, the Department of Justice.

The counterrevolution will be televised (on Facebook). Organizations endorsing Hillary Clinton add 8.9 million likes to HfA's 2.5 million likes. Her unions have 748,000 likes, her major organizations have 4.2 million likes, and her closely aligned (c) (4)'s have 4.0 million likes, numbers dwarfed by the Facebook fans of her endorsing celebrities.

Treat their Facebook pages as television stations. Secure permission to post HfA-produced memes and videos on their pages.

Pay to boost those ads to their fans and friends in targeted states. Expand HfA's reach, impose message discipline, and save resources on campaign communications."

Our meeting lasted roughly 40 minutes, enough time to cover most of the above points, watch a Crying Diaper Baby video and exchange contact information. Podesta asked questions, took notes and suggested he would put me in touch with one of the campaign's social media gurus. He also asked me to send him a copy of my 2008 memo to Howard Paster about how to avoid a Carter–Kennedy style convention wipeout.

In the weeks that followed, I resumed e-mail exchanges with Dan Schwerin, Hillary's speechwriter, Amanda Rentera, the campaign's political director, and Nikki Budinski, its labor liaison. I was also called by Jason Rosenbaum who was following up on the Podesta meeting. And I managed to contribute and raise enough money that I started getting e-mails meant for Hillary for America's finance committee members.

Despite this, I was still plagued by doubts about the campaign. Specifically, I was worried that no one was taking Trump seriously or even considered him much of a threat at all. So I began working on a "red team strategy" memo—an exercise designed to look at the battle space from the perspective of one's opponents—and based on my own analysis of a mid-April battleground poll. My work product consisted of two elements and was e-mailed to John Podesta on April 21.

In "Trump's Non-Battleground State Scenario," seven assumptions were detailed. The first four were straightforward: Trump would be the GOP nominee, continue to engage 56 million Twitter followers and Facebook fans per week, expand his focus to white working class Democrats, knew the Electoral College was stacked against him and would pick an establishment figure from Ohio or Florida. Four out of five wasn't bad for an armchair strategist—Trump picked an establishment Republican from Indiana, Governor Mike Pence. But assumptions six and seven and their rationales were where the rubber met the road:

Assumption 6: However, Trump will NOT run a traditional battleground state strategy. Instead he will attempt to win the popular vote. By focusing on the top media markets, specifically the top markets located in the biggest Deep Blue and Battleground States, his 757 can hit each of them four times in the 110 days between the RNC Convention and Election Day.

> Rationale A: White working class Democrats will be Trump's targets of opportunity. His message about jobs, trade deals, immigration and political correctness will resonate with the most marginalized of those voters. And the highest concentrations of those non-college Democratic voters can be found in the biggest Deep Blue and Battleground states.

Rationale B: Cutting President Obama's margins in the states containing those top 25 media markets by just 25 percent puts Trump within striking distance of winning the popular vote. More importantly, it places him within 120,000 votes of winning Ohio, Florida, North Carolina and Virginia.

Rationale C: Achieving a 25% reduction in Obama's margin from 2012 is not all that difficult. Trump would be trimming the president's vote tally by only 2.5% in Pennsylvania, 0.6% in Ohio, 0.4% in Florida, 2.3% in Colorado, 1.8% in Virginia and 1.1% in North Carolina.

Rationale D: In the biggest Deep Blue states, a 25% reduction in Obama's margin from 2012 would not alter the results—the Democratic ticket would still win—but it would lower its popular vote tally by 2 million. You would see a shift of 670,000 votes in California, 410,000 in New York, 215,000 in Illinois, 180,000 in Massachusetts, 170,000 in Maryland, 120,000 in Washington State and 113,000 in Michigan.

Assumption 7: Trump's appeal to working class white Democrats only works in a vacuum. His ability to trim Obama's margins by 25% relies on the Democratic ticket ignoring this key constituency and being surprised by a nontraditional strategy.

The "red team strategy" memo then listed five counterstrategies ranging from starting early to reconnect with working class Democrats, using prime time convention programming, retooling Hillary Clinton's narrative, picking a running mate that appealed to populists and progressives, making Donald Trump the riskiest choice for working class families and encouraging President Obama and Vice President Biden to campaign in the top 25 media markets in the Deep Blue and Battleground States.

But the core of the "red team strategy" was an interactive spreadsheet that listed those top 25 Democratic media markets and their respective states.[32] For comparison purposes, it listed the raw vote margins for each state for 2004, 2008 and 2012 and provided the total each year for the 18 states and the District of Columbia. And it showed that the Kerry–Edwards campaign lost those states by 1.4 million votes in 2008; Obama–Biden won them by 18.7 million in 2008 and by 9.3 million in 2012.

The spreadsheet also contained the percentage margin in 2012—Obama's percentage minus Romney's percentage—in each state and the District of Columbia. It allowed the user to enter the current margin according to either the *RealClear Politics* average or the 538 polling projections and a percentage increase/decrease was automatically calculated. So it became obvious, instantaneously, which state Donald Trump was cutting deeply into the margin that Barack Obama had won or, in the case of Missouri, lost the state by and by what percentage.

The assumption behind the "red team strategy" was that Trump would seek to cut the 2012 margin by 25 percent by repeatedly traveling to the largest media markets in those 19 states. Such a squeezing of the margins would, in effect, reduce Hillary Clinton's tally in the popular vote from the biggest, bluest states—and provide a warning sign to Podesta and, presumably, to her campaign manager and senior staff.

Hillary Clinton' margins would shrink as compared to Obama's margins, inevitably, because of higher than average numbers of voters who were undecided, a significantly higher percentage of third party voters in 2016 than in 2012 and Trump's aggressive appeals to working class Democrats.

Those undecided would break for or against Clinton in the final weeks of the campaign but would be influenced by two pivot points—the selection of her running mate and the Democratic convention. The strength of the third-party candidacies would shrink somewhat. But Trump's appeals to working class Democrats could not be allowed to go unchallenged.

In that Tarrance/Lake battleground poll (April 17–20), Hillary Clinton drew support from 37 percent of whites, 91 percent from Blacks and 52 percent from Hispanics. Among the unemployed, she drew 47 percent with 20 percent undecided! Union households split 54 percent for Clinton and 37 percent for Trump. Retirees, aged 65 or older, and White seniors were a mixed bag.

So, at least to me, the real battle space—as opposed to the battleground states—was white voters, a demographic that was neither monolithic nor entirely monopolized by the GOP. Finding ways to chip away at Trump's support among women, particularly white working class women, was necessary. Driving down his support among the unemployed, union households and retirees was not just necessary. It was vital.

Every 45 days or so, I e-mailed Podesta an updated spread sheet with the most recent *RealClear Politics* state polling averages, how their margins impacted the projected voter turnout and how their vote totals compared with Obama's in 2012 and 2008. The e-mails contained a brief report on Trump's travels to those 25 media markets and the 18 states plus the District of Columbia they covered. As the November election neared, my e-mails became more and more frantic.

Oddly, while my request for John Podesta to meet with Leo Hindery to discuss a significant contribution to the Democratic National Committee was released by Wikileaks, my "red team strategy" e-mails never were.

Perhaps Vladimir Putin shared them with Donald Trump's campaign?

Just kidding, Vlad!

CHAPTER 34

PIVOT POINTS

Six months after walking across the stage with my [journeyman] diploma, I was laid off due to a lack of work. Since that time, I have had to leave my apartment and move back in with my parents because I could not afford rent, bills or food on my own. I sleep on a lazy-boy chair in my parents' two-bedroom apartment ... I am one of the fortunate ones, however, I am single and still have a family who was willing to take me in.

Anthony's Unemployment Story

As the Michigan primary approached, Hillary Clinton's speechwriter Dan Schwerin and I exchanged another series of e-mails that proved to be as disheartening to me as some of our prior correspondence. It began with my assertion that "Brooklyn doesn't get the value" of working class Democrats. I poured salt on the wound by adding, "But Trump does. And so does Sanders." Brooklyn, where her campaign headquarter was located, was my shorthand way of blaming the entire campaign, not an individual and certainly not Schwerin himself.

Schwerin admitted that the Clinton campaign hadn't cracked the code, their candidate hadn't connected emotionally with them and they were searching for ways to unlock the emotions of Hillary and those working class Democrats. He pushed back on the idea that Brooklyn did not care. To prove his point, he included a link to a YouTube clip of Secretary Clinton talking about bringing jobs back and hollowed out communities.

The clip reinforced both his point and mine. Hillary was talking *about* "hollowed out communities" as if the people in them did not exist. She was not speaking *to* the working class Democrats who lived there. If she were, she would have been *amongst* them, not standing all alone behind a podium. And her phrases "love and kindness," "work together" and "breaking down barriers" were as tired as her delivery was.

It was so unlike the Hillary Clinton I knew.

In fact, at the debate the night before our e-mail exchange, Hillary Clinton answered a question from a Latina whose husband had been deported. It was her singularly best moment of the night. The woman was, by any definition, working class. Hillary connected with her on a very basic level—as a human being, as a wife and as a mother.

I wrote back to Schwerin. "That's where Hillary is at her best. It is also where she draws strength and energy from those she meets. So, her campaign has to put her in places where her natural empathy connects with voters—their living rooms and kitchens, their schools and churches, their work places and shopping centers—and where their natural affection for her raises *her* energy level."

"Give them a chance to SEE how much she cares about them. Forget the nuances of language for a moment. Concentrate instead on the compelling PICTURES that news crews and social media can make go viral. I know that's not what speechwriters are supposed to do. But you're the one guy who can ask: what [should be] the backdrop and foreground for this message? You can ask: How can these carefully crafted words be amplified by the picture[?] And you can ask: How, if the voice conveys energy and it does, how can Hillary be energized by the people closest to her?"

To a campaign built around events-in-a-box—the same podium, staging, risers and backdrops filled with sign-waving supporters in every location—I was speaking heresies. Hillary Clinton wasn't about to give up her podium. And Brooklyn wasn't about to demand that she do so just to connect with a "demo slice" that wasn't part of their "rising America electorate."

Hillary Clinton lost Michigan to Bernie Sanders by 50 percent to 48 percent. And then from late March to early April, she lost seven caucus states by 50 points (or more) and then lost the Wisconsin primary by 16 points. Her wins in New York, Connecticut, Delaware, Maryland and Pennsylvania in late April and early May made it mathematically impossible for Bernie Sanders to secure Democratic nomination. That old delegate selection matrix was driving the delegate allocations. Sanders simply could not outperform Hillary Clinton in the remaining states by large enough margins to reverse her lead in both pledged and super delegates. It was game over.

Brooklyn never found the key to unlock the emotions of working class Democrats, or those of their own candidate. Now time was growing short. Once the nomination was locked up, there were only three pivot points where a presidential campaign—any presidential campaign—can make a significant course correction: the selection of a running mate, the management and messaging of their national convention and how the undecided voters broke after the presidential debates concluded.

Each of those pivot points offered a chance to influence the campaign's decision-makers. And, since I had a personal interest in the vice presidential selection process (my old roommate was reportedly being vetted), I began by urging labor leaders, women's rights advocates, progressives and even senior members of the Clinton campaign staff to use the selection process as a way to solve its growing problem with white working class Democrats and, at the same time, avoid a massive rejection by white males generally.

In a cover e-mail to those three dozen leaders, I explained that "according to the latest Battleground Survey, Hillary Clinton trails Donald Trump by 37 points among married white males (61% to 24% with 15% undecided). So the attached analysis explores the depth of that challenge, the quick fixes that will only backfire, and a strategy to shrink that margin.

"I am acutely aware of the politically incorrect ground I dare to tread. White married men *are* a privileged population. Their perceptions of lost jobs, lost opportunities, and lost status, however, *are not* imagined slights but a slow-moving reality. And, yes, some of them are racists, anti-semites, homophobes and misogynists. But the overwhelming majority of them are not."

I asked them to keep "an open mind about this key demographic. For to win next November, we will have to change enough minds to pare that 37 point margin to fewer than 25 points. And we cannot do that if we write them off completely."

The accompanying analysis was brutally honest and began by asserting that Hillary Clinton was the bete noire of married white males. In a tightening race against Donald Trump, their antipathy was more than problematic. The three-page analysis continued:

> "In the most recent Battleground Poll, Clinton trailed Donald Trump among white married men by 24% to 62%. She trailed him by 30% to 66% among no longer married white men. Those two demographics accounted for 27.8 percent of the nationwide sample. Losing more than a quarter of the popular vote by 36 to 38 points is a prescription for disaster.

> The only white males Clinton won were unmarried. She beat Trump by 50% to 36% among single white men. They represented only 7.4% of the sample.

REVENGE OF AMERICA'S UNEMPLOYED

But Hillary is not alone. President Obama lost white men by 35% to 62% to Mitt Romney in 2012—a 27 point shellacking but ten points better than Hillary is faring right now. To be clear, every Democratic nominee since 1972 has lost white males. So it would be easy for Democrats to write off one-third of the electorate as a lost cause.

But a deeper look at the historical data and the 2012 exit polls in key states suggests that would be a massive mistake. In fact, winning at least 37.5% of white men is doable and, more importantly, a prerequisite for Hillary Clinton to win the popular vote and the Electoral College."

In every exit poll from 1972 to 2012, the Democratic ticket lost white males. But it was the margin of those losses that determined if the ticket won or lost the presidency. When the margin exceeded 24 percent, Democrats lost every time except in 2012. They were blown away (and so were down ballot candidates) when the margin exceeded 35 percent as it did in 1972 with George McGovern and in 1980 with Jimmy Carter.

Democrats won when the margin closed to less than 16 percent. It is how Barack Obama won in 2008, Bill Clinton won in 1996 and 1992 (with help from Ross Perrot) and Carter won in 1976. As noted above, Obama beat Romney in 2012 when the margin was 27 points based on a historically high turnout among African-American, Latino and Asian voters. But Carter lost to Reagan in 1980 and Michael Dukakis lost to Bush in 1988 when the margin was 27 points.

Shrinking the national margin to less than 25 points, that is, losing white men by 37.5 percent to 62.5 percent or less, was mission critical for Hillary Clinton. But the national spread is not nearly as important as the margins in the battleground states. For not every state tracks national trends. For example, the margin for the Obama–Biden ticket among white men was 12 points in New York and 14 points in California. It was 32 points in Florida.

"Across the Rust Belt that Donald Trump intends to target, the Obama/Biden ticket lost white men by 14 points in Wisconsin, 17 points in Michigan, 21 points in Pennsylvania, and 26 points in Ohio. In what were battleground states in 2012, the Obama/Biden ticket lost white males by 6 points in New Hampshire, 14 points in Colorado and Iowa, 17 points in New Mexico, 22 points in Nevada, 30 points in Virginia yet it still won those six states. In North Carolina, a 38 point margin among white men flipped the state for the Romney/Ryan ticket."

To me, the ultimate test any potential vice presidential nominee faced was this: Did they help Secretary Clinton narrow those margins sufficiently to prevail next November, particularly in the battleground states?

And that was where the analysis began to tread on politically incorrect ground by asking three pointed questions:

"**As the Democratic nominee for vice president, can Julian Castro or Tom Perez increase Latino participation next November?** Absolutely. But by how much?

To answer that question we need to know three baseline numbers—Latino turnout, the Latino partisan split, and the Latino vote for the Democratic ticket. In each instance, it is more of a highly educated guess than a hard and fast number.

In 2012, the popular vote was 129.6 million. If the 2012 exit polls were accurate, then 12.9 million Latinos voted. They split their vote 71% for Obama and 29% for Romney. President Obama received 9.2 million Latino votes.

If Castro or Perez could increase Latino turnout by 4% this November, then the Latino total vote would grow to 13.4 million. And, if the partisan split remained 71% to 29%, Secretary

Clinton would receive 9.5 million votes, an increase of 300,000 votes nationwide.

What if Cory Booker or Deval Patrick were nominated? Would that increase African American participation next November? Again, the answer is absolutely.

In 2012, the exit polls indicate that 16.8 million African Americans voted. They split 93% for Obama to 7% for Romney. President Obama received 15.6 million African American votes.

If Senator Booker or former Governor Patrick could increase African American turnout by 4%, its total vote would climb to 17.5 million. If the partisan split remained 93% to 7%, then Secretary Clinton would receive 16.2 million votes, an increase of 600,000 votes nationwide.

But what if Senators Elizabeth Warren, Tim Kaine or Sherrod Brown were on the ticket? Would that matter? Certainly.

In 2012, the exit polls suggested that 93 million whites voted. They split 39% for Obama to 61% for Romney. President Obama received 36.3 million white votes.

If Warren, Kaine or Brown could increase white turnout by 4 percent over 2012, then its total vote would be 96.7 million. If the partisan split in 2012 remained the same, 39% to 61%, then Secretary Clinton would win 37.7 million white votes, an increase of 1.4 million votes."

The likely increases in Hillary Clinton's popular vote were 300,000 . . . 600,000 . . . 1,400,000 when a Latino, an African-American or a white running mate increases turnout by 4 percent and the 2012 partisan split remained the same. However, those *increases* were specious—superficially plausible, but actually wrong—for no running mate regardless of their race can, or can be expected to, increase national turnout by 4 percent.

Those *increases* were also spurious. The inherent fraud is that the size of the demographic blocs drives those numbers, not the appeal of any individual. And they are misleading to the extent that such sophistry moves us away from Democratic unity and toward racial division.

"Selecting a running mate is not a numbers game," I argued. "Never has been. Never should be. When it comes right down to it, there are only two criteria that matter."

"First, does the prospective nominee have the credibility to be the president of the United States if, God forbid, the 25th Amendment must be invoked?

Second, is he or she compatible with the party's nominee— can she or he put aside their own ego and ambitions to work closely and effectively for four or even eight years?"

Doing the math just showed how inane the arguments about age, gender, race, religion and region can become. When it came right down to it, the numbers were not relevant. Selecting the next Teddy Roosevelt, Harry S Truman or Lyndon Baines Johnson was the ultimate test. And in all likelihood, it weighed most heavily on the Democrat's decider-in-chief: Hillary Clinton herself. What she needed from a running mate was the tensile strength to match her own.

Married white males preferred Donald Trump over Hillary Clinton by 37 points in the mid-April battleground survey for a reason. It was why every subsequent poll had Trump gaining on Clinton. When more than a quarter of the electorate was splitting 61 percent to 24 percent against her, all the alarms in Hillary's Brooklyn headquarters should have been blaring.

Sadly, their natural reaction was to say, "Screw 'em. We can make up the difference, just as President Obama did, by pumping up turnout among African-Americans, Latinos, Asians and Millennials." And yet, that approach would only get them so far. The Obama–Biden ticket won in spite of losing white males by 27 points.

But losing by 37 points? That's unprecedented. It is a wider margin than either George McGovern faced in 1972 or Jimmy Carter endured in 1984. And there simply are not enough minority and millennial voters to close so wide a gap.

The analysis closed by arguing that Hillary Clinton could "ill afford to write off married white men. Instead she has to compete head-to-head with Trump for their votes. And she can do so by asking them a simple, direct question, "How do YOU define courage?"

> "Make married white men define courage. Theirs. Their father's. Their mother's. Their grandparents'. Make them define for their own sons and daughters what real courage entails.

> For courage, real courage, cannot be defined by gender. Real courage defies gender. It always has and always will. But, in the 2016 presidential contest, real courage is what separates the candidates.

> Hillary Clinton has a warrior's spirit—a compassion for those struggling to break down barriers, an inner confidence to prevail against all odds and over all enemies, a simple but strict and yet explicit code of honor, a willingness to be held accountable for the policies she proposes, and the fortitude to never quit even when the prospects are so dire that other men and women would do so in a heartbeat.

> By contrast, Donald Trump had the spirit of a schoolyard bully—a preference for picking on and abusing the weakest, a narcissism that masked a deeply seeded inferiority complex, a code of omertà about his associates, taxes and business practices, a penchant for avoiding responsibility and hiding behind

lame excuses, and a long streak of cowardice that, unconscionably, conflated a boarding school for brats with the Hanoi Hilton's torture of American prisoners of war.

Make married white men [choose]: Clinton's courage or Trump's cowardice.

Presented with a challenge to his manhood, Donald Trump will, no doubt, make this race about anatomy. And Hillary Clinton's surrogates should attack his premise.

For hand size is not the measure of a president. Tensile strength is. Brass balls have more tensile strength than nerf balls. Or, as one White House aide said about Harry Truman after he called on coal miners to end their nationwide strike, 'you could hear his balls clank.' And married white men know that nerf balls can't clank."

Married white men also needed to know that their children and grandchildren will be the victims of Trump's narcissistic rages if he were to be elected. His vacuous policies and vicious politics may be momentarily entertaining for some of them. But like all reality shows, they are only a diversion from the disparities and indignities of daily life they faced.

If they have no hope of building a better life for themselves, what legacy can they pass on to their kids and grand babies? What can they point to with pride and say, "I did that. I made this. Or I built that."? What, in fact, are the monuments to their lives . . . save the faces formed by their own DNA?

For those married white men come from a long line of nation builders. In steel, concrete and glass, in pipes, wires and fiberoptic cables, in wood, sheetrock and plastic, they and their ancestors built a nation, a nation of 323 million people. In constitutions, statutes and regulations, in commercial contracts, music sheets and newspapers, in books, computer programs and apps, they built a nation that the rest of the world envies.

They built that nation working side-by-side with African-American, Latino, Asian and Native American men and women. And each of those married white men had a partner who built this nation with their own strength and sacrifice, drive and determination.

Given a choice between courage or cowardice, I believed that enough married white men would choose courage. Given a choice between building a wall between nations and becoming a nation of builders once again, I believed enough of them would chose to be nation builders.

And I believed that Hillary Clinton should choose a white male as her running mate, one who had the tensile strength to be the president in the event of a tragedy, one who could relate to the tough guys who had had her back in 2008, one who could deliver a key battleground state. And I wasn't shy about making the case for my old roommate, Ohio Senator Sherrod Brown.

In a *Huffington Post* piece published on June 28, I explained how the Obama and Romney campaigns spent $150 million on television ads in Ohio, how the state was inundated with 58,253 ads and how, despite saving the state's auto industry, Obama beat Romney by only 166,214 votes out of 5.6 million cast. Ohio was a flip-of-the-coin state.

"Ohio: The 150 Million Dollar Question in 2016," not surprisingly, focused on working class Democrats. It argued,

> "Ohio's working class Democratic males don't give a big hoot about issues. They mostly want to know their candidate cares about them, values the work they do, and sees them as 'family'.

> To put this into perspective, according to What Went Wrong, a report by the Brookings Institute, Ohio has seen more than a 50% decline in manufacturing jobs since 1970. The once bucolic mini-city of Mansfield has lost 29% of its manufacturing jobs. Cleveland and Elyria have lost 42.5% of their

manufacturing jobs. Ditto for Canton and Massillon at 44.1%
and Akron has lost 33.2% of its manufacturing jobs."

No one was more familiar with those pernicious trends than Sherrod
Brown. He had represented *all* of those working class Democratic bastions
and had fought for those towns and towns like them his entire career.

Brown wrote the book, literally, on job-killing trade deals "The Myths
of Free Trade." He led the fights against CAFTA, Fast Track and the Trans
Pacific Partnership. He fought Larry Summers' apotheosis as Chairman
of the Federal Reserve and pushed hard for Janet Yellen's more focused
approach to unemployment. So, if any Democrat could appeal to working
males, in Ohio and across the Rust Belt, Sherrod Brown would.

But "coulda, woulda, shoulda" did not much matter in the final
analysis. By the end of the Republican National Convention in Cleveland,
Ohio, the $150-million question had been asked and answered.

Hillary Clinton selected Senator Tim Kaine of Virginia as her running mate.

CHAPTER 35

AMERICA'S INVESTMENT BANK

I am NO longer considered working middle class;
I live in poverty ... I can no longer support, live or
feed myself. I find myself going to the food banks. It
is very degrading. I have been working for 23 years
and I have nothing to show for it.

Sheri's Unemployment Story

As the presidential campaigns turned toward their national conventions in late July, millions of Americans were feeling left behind and left out. The infamous U-6 had dipped to 9.6 percent, a 1/10 of a point downward shift. The BLS was gleefully reporting that employers had added 287,000 jobs in June calling it "a very strong figure."

Even Leo Hindery's *real* unemployment rate had decreased to 9.6 percent, matching up with the U-6 rate for the first time since he began publishing his monthly analysis. But the "important note" at the bottom of his July e-mail still read,

"In addition to the 15.4 million Real Employed Persons [on] June 30, there are another 4.3 million workers who, while saying they want jobs, have not looked for work in the past twelve months. Solely because they haven't looked, these workers are not included among the marginally attached workers; if included June's Real Unemployment Rate of 9.6% substantially increases to 12.0%."

Hindery's analysis put total real unemployment at 19.7 million Americans. Those 20 million Americans were not alone in feeling left behind and left out. Millions of other Americans had dropped out of the workforce entirely. They had stopped looking for jobs that were not there to be found and were, consequently, uncounted by any unemployment report.

As they had in 2008, 2010, 2012 and 2014 elections, those tens of millions of unemployed, underemployed and uncounted Americans—and the family members who had experienced their isolation, frustration and depression first hand—faced very hard, very stark choices. To vote or not to vote was their first question. And, if they did vote, which of the four party's nominees would they support.

Donald Trump had locked up his party's nomination in May but many in the Republican establishment kept hoping against hope that he might self-destruct before their convention opened in Cleveland, Ohio. Hillary Clinton nailed down enough pledged delegates and commitments from super delegates to be the Democratic Party's presumptive nominee in May, too, but Bernie Sanders kept campaigning hard through the final primaries and caucus states and kept threatening to take his revolution to the floor of the Democratic National Convention.

But trouble was brewing. A bidding war was about to break out over an issue that could, if handled correctly, convince many of those jobless Americans to go vote . . . and vote for a candidate that they did not particularly like or even trust.

Ironically, all but one of the active presidential candidates shared a common belief. From Hillary Clinton to Bernie Sanders (who had only suspended his campaign), from Donald Trump to Jill Stein, the Green Party candidate, each had proposed major investments in infrastructure. The libertarian, Gary Johnson, was the one exception, although even he had once supported a private-private partnership between Koch Industries, Inc. and New Mexico to widen a state highway.

Yet, it was the contrast between their various plans that first drew my attention. Back in September 2015, Hillary Clinton had issued an infrastructure policy paper that dedicated $25 billion to an investment bank and allocated another $250 billion to fund infrastructure projects over five years. Two months later, Bernie Sanders proposed a trillion-dollar infrastructure plan, a plan that relied on taxing Wall Street transactions. Both candidates had made rebuilding our crumbling infrastructure a key point in their stump speeches and a wedge issue in their debates.

Infrastructure, as an issue, could be weaponized. Clinton could—and occasionally did—use the issue to show how Sanders' pie-in-the-sky plan would never be enacted. Sanders could—and often did—use the issue to hammer Clinton on her ties to Wall Street and her small-potatoes approach.

And yet, infrastructure was also an issue that could, literally and figuratively, bridge the differences between the two Democratic campaigns. Leo Hindery, by now a personal friend and a stalwart supporter of the Union of Unemployed, had been advocating for an infrastructure bank for a decade. His plan differed in substantial detail from both the Clinton and Sanders' plans. His approach called for an infrastructure bank that, by using the leverage of $150 billion in government loan guarantees, could generate up to $1.5 trillion in public and private investments and employ millions of Americans on the infrastructure projects the bank funded.

After meeting with John Podesta and discussing with the Hillary for America issues team focused on infrastructure, Hindery became the go-to-guy on what was now being called America's Infrastructure Bank. His patience and persuasiveness paid off. In mid-June, he was asked by Podesta to share his approach, directly, with Bernie Sanders. He did so. And a day or so later, he shared it with Jeff Merkley, the only senator to have endorsed Sanders and a member of the Democratic Platform Drafting Committee.

Within a week, both Senators Sanders and Merkley had signed off on the language suggested by Hindery. The Clinton and Sanders folks on the drafting committee adopted,

> "Democrats will also create an independent, national infra-structure bank that will support critical infrastructure improvements. This bank will provide loans and other finan-cial assistance for investments in energy, water, broadband, transportation, and multi-modal infrastructure projects. Democrats will continue to support the interest tax exemption on municipal bonds and will work to establish a permanent version of Build America Bonds as an additional tool to encour-age infrastructure investment by state and local governments."

Or, as Hindery put in an e-mail to those involved, "in a way, the Bank's first 'infrastructure project' was bridging a previously unbridgeable divide."

Three days earlier, Hillary Clinton had upped the ante. In a lengthy economic speech delivered in Raleigh, North Carolina, she had pledged:

> "In my first 100 days as president, I will work with both par-ties to pass a comprehensive plan to create the next generation of good jobs. Now the heart of my plan will be the biggest investment in American infrastructure in decades, including establishing an infrastructure bank that will bring private sec-tor dollars off the sidelines and put them to work here....
>
> We can create millions of good paying jobs while preparing America to compete and win in the global economy.
>
> So let's set these big national goals. And I know how important it is to rebuild our roads, our bridges, and our airports, but

we have more work to do. Let's build better. And let's connect every household to broadband by the year 2020."

Ironically, behind the scenes, I had been pushing the concept of "A New Nation of Builders and America's Infrastructure Bank" since sending the "red team strategy" memos to Podesta back in mid-April. I had turned the idea into a *Huffington Post* piece that Podesta urged Leo Hindery and I should publish, jointly, with instructions to take a hard shot at Donald Trump. It was also the topic of an 80-minute conversation with Lissa Muscatine, who was working on Bill Clinton's convention speech when we spoke. She took copious notes and produced an *eyes only* memo for Hillary Clinton.

Faint echoes of the ". . . Nation of Builders . . ." concept were heard in Hillary's acceptance speech at the convention in Philadelphia. And that *Huffington Post* piece, co-authored by Leo Hindery, Mike Wessel[33] and myself, finally appeared on August 18. Its key paragraph read,

> "But to continue to 'secure the Blessings of Liberty to our-selves and our Posterity' we must continually strengthen the ties that bind us together as a nation. And especially in this national election year, with the challenges ahead and the deep economic divides that still exist in the country, we must not let so-called 'hard-edge nationalism' divide us by political party or by race, religion or region …

> If we are to continue to celebrate the absolute power of a free people to forge an American dream for the families and if we are to stay a nation of builders, then we need to take on the hard work of strengthening these infrastructure ties that bind us together — our roads and bridges; our railroads, airports

and seaports; and our electrical grid and water treatment plants."

Those 19.7 million unemployed, underemployed and uncounted Americans, finally, had a decision to make. So did the millions of laid-off Americans who had found work but at a fraction of what they had made before the Great Recession struck. So did those additional millions of Americans who had been "prematurely retired" from the workforce over the previous eight years. And so did the family members who had watched them struggle with the loneliness, the sense of isolation, the loss of income and assets, the loss of self-esteem and self-confidence. For in this economic tragedy, few were immune to its most destructive forces.

That decision offered no shades of grey; it was black and white. They could waste their votes on third party candidates who'd never win, vote for Hillary Clinton who had pledged to make the "biggest investment in new, good paying jobs since World War II", vote for Donald Trump who said in a Fox Business Network interview that he would invest $500 billion in infrastructure or they could stay home.

Would we be a Nation of Builders? Or a nation of developers?

In millions of jobless households, that decision had been years in the making.

CHAPTER 36

A PLURALITY THRESHOLD

I'm 58, and I'm terrified that I will run out of unemployment, and that the Governor of our state, Maine, who is a lunatic, will pass his law saying that each person can be helped ONCE by their towns through general assistance. That leaves me only one choice, doesn't it? Homelessness. The end result of that is death by inches. Me? I am planning to move to Washington DC if that time comes. I'll sleep on the doorstep of my Senators ... I won't go quietly. I'll go loud and vocal telling the media everything I can to stop it from happening to anyone else.

Eleanor's Unemployment Story

Given the sky-high negatives of the two major party candidates, the two third-party candidates were drawing double-digit levels of support in four-way horse race surveys in mid-July 2016. The *ABC News/Washington Post* poll had the two minor party candidates at 13 percent; the *NBC News/Wall Street Journal* poll put them at 17 percent.

The Libertarian Party nominated Gary Johnson, the former GOP governor from New Mexico. The Green Party picked Jill Stein. So, for the first time since Ralph Nader ran as the Green Party nominee in 2000 and flipped Florida to George Bush, the third party vote was poised to play a significant role in a presidential election: it would cut into the margins the Democratic nominee needed in those 19 big blue and battleground states listed in the "red team strategy."

How deeply would the third party vote cut into those margins, and which way would the undecided voters break? Those questions could not be answered, completely, until the final weeks of the campaign. But there was a way to make an educated guess as to what was likely to happen.

Back in 1992, while working for the AFT, I devised a Plurality Threshold to better understand the threat from Ross Perot. I shared it with David Wilhelm, who had led Bill Clinton's campaign in the primaries, and with other friends in the Little Rock headquarters. In a chaotic and confusing year, the Plurality Threshold helped us see through "the fog of war."

Right before the Democratic Convention and his "withdrawal" from the race, Ross Perot led both Bill Clinton and George Bush in 21 states with 308 Electoral College votes (ECVs). When Perot returned to the race in October, he went on to rack up between 24.3 percent to 30.7 percent of the vote in 11 states, mostly states with three, four or five electoral votes. In larger states like Oregon and Washington, he ended up with 25.1 percent and 24.3 percent, respectively.

Perot was a major player in 1992—he pushed the Plurality Threshold down so far that Bill Clinton beat an incumbent, war-winning president by 370 to 168 ECVs.

So, what the hell is a Plurality Threshold?

It's a simple equation. The Plurality Threshold equals a simple majority (50 percent) minus the third parties combined percentage of the vote divided by two. Or, PT = 50% − (Third Party % + Fourth Party %)/2.

By Labor Day 2016, Gary Johnson was still getting 7.4 percent and Jill Stein was drawing 3.1 percent. Their combined vote of 10.5 percent meant that the Plurality Threshold was 44.75 percent, nationally.

The Plurality Threshold varied from state to state. With the third-party candidates now drawing between 7 percent and 15 percent, sums that would shrink or grow depending on the state and the state of the contest, neither major party candidate could win an absolute majority of the vote in most battleground states. Non-battleground states were a different story.

There was, however, a quirk in how the Plurality Threshold worked. The system *was* rigged, mathematically speaking, in such a multi-candidate race. For every percentage point gained over the Plurality Threshold, the leading candidate doubled the distance between them and their nearest opponent. So come-from-behind victories in a four-way race were nearly impossible—too many voters were locked down too early—*if* and *only if* the leading contender was *above* the Plurality Threshold. Even then, a campaign had to keep an eye on how the undecided were breaking.

The Plurality Threshold was, after all, a moving target subject to the ebb and flow of politics—a major gaffe, an opposition research factoid that makes headlines, an October surprise that moves numbers or a candidate having a really bad night in a debate all have the potential to set the threshold adrift. So, in order to win the election, it was imperative to get above the threshold as quickly as possible and build an irreversible lead in as many battleground states as possible.

In the darkest blue states, Secretary Clinton was either at or above the Plurality Threshold in polls released in August. Even though Johnson and Stein were drawing between 7 percent to 15 percent in states like New York, California, Pennsylvania, Wisconsin and California, Hillary Clinton could bank on the 247 ECVs from the 19 dark blue states identified in the "red team strategy." But there were caveats.

Because of the third party's votes in those dark blue states, the margin (or spread) between Clinton and Trump would be much smaller than between Obama and Romney. That would make for a much narrower victory (or, possibly, even a slight loss) in the nation-wide popular vote.

Beyond mere bragging rights, expanding the margin in those dark blue state alters, mathematically, the national horse race and tracking poll numbers in the closing weeks. That, in turn, tends to influence the 10 to 12 percent of late deciding voters who make up their minds in the final days. It is a momentum game at that stage because everyone loves a winner. If the undecideds break for a candidate, they can usually put that candidate over the Plurality Threshold in the battleground states, the states needed to win an Electoral College victory.

Given that those dark blue states seldom see a Democratic presidential campaign save for an occasional touch-and-go to do a fundraiser, adding a message event to those stops would help with Democratic turnout. And conducting a social media blitz that connected with working class Democrats could also expand the margin in those dark blue states.

In the traditional battleground states—Iowa, New Hampshire, Ohio, Nevada, Florida, Colorado, Virginia, North Carolina—the picture was mixed. Hillary Clinton was three points above the Plurality Threshold in Colorado where Johnson and Stein had amassed 23 percent of the vote. In Virginia, with help from Tim Kaine, she was 3.5 points above the threshold as the third-party candidates combined for 11 percent of the vote. So, those two states' 22 ECVs could be added to Hillary Clinton's tally. That put her at 269 ECVs and one electoral vote shy of winning the Electoral College.

In early September, the Plurality Threshold was 47.5 percent in Nevada, 46 percent in New Hampshire and Florida, 45.5 percent in Iowa, 45 percent in North Carolina and 44 percent in Ohio. Trump and Clinton were locked in very competitive races. Neither candidate polled above the Plurality Threshold in any of those states.

And yet, in those six states, Hillary Clinton had a distinct advantage in field organization, big data, accumulated rating points from paid advertising, and an impressive "Get Out The Vote" operation. So a final 96-hour campaign swing through their major media markets would help. By then, the Clinton campaign should, hopefully, be blowing past the Plurality Threshold by two or three points *and*, simultaneously, pushing Hillary's tally into the stratospheric range of 332 electoral votes.

The Plurality Threshold, however, could also identify outliers. States like Georgia, Arkansas, Arizona and Missouri whose 43 electoral votes could produce a thumping, to borrow a phrase from President George Bush, that Trump and the Republicans would not soon forget. With an aggressive turnout effort among African Americans and Latinos and a series of reminders to white working class Democrats what the GOP has done *to* them and *for* the wealthiest Americans over the years, Hillary Clinton could swing those states into her column just by adding 3 percent to her current base of support in each state.

If she had done so, Hillary Clinton would have ended up with 375 ECVs to Trump's 163 ECVs. And that was the Trump *thumpin'* he so richly deserved.

Unfortunately, as September rolled on and the October surprises came and went—the Russian hacks, the Wikileaks e-mail dumps, the sordid Trump tape and FBI Director Comey's letters roiled the news cycles—the Plurality Threshold showed an increasingly competitive race.

The *Washington Post* teamed up with Survey Monkey to survey all 50 states. The results of the poll's 74,000 interviews were released on September 6. It suggested that the presidential "campaign could flip several red and blue states from their longtime loyalties." The Plurality Threshold, using the poll's own results, indicated that Trump was *above* the threshold by more than 2.5 percent in 20 states with 143 electoral votes. Clinton, by contrast, was *above* the threshold in 17 states with 210 electoral votes. In

Nevada, New Hampshire and Pennsylvania, her campaign was less than 1.4 percent from breaking through the threshold.

More problematic, Secretary Clinton was more than 2.5 percent or more *below* the threshold in Arizona, Georgia, Iowa, North Carolina, Ohio, Texas and Wisconsin. She was *below* the threshold by 1.5 percent to 2.4 percent in Colorado, Florida, Maine and Michigan. None of those numbers were chiseled in stone and the Clinton campaign was making steady progress in some of those states. But so was Trump's campaign, particularly in Arizona, Texas and Georgia.

What is important to remember is that a presidential campaign is always fluid. The polling numbers, the algorithms, the projections—yes, even the Plurality Thresholds—change. To rely on any single number is sheer folly. When 120 to 140 million Americans start voting, no pundit or prognosticator or pollster or seasoned poll can truly predict what will happen. No one is 100 percent clairvoyant.

The men and women running for office, their staffs and supporters are prone to make mistakes—to err is human. All those equations and surveys and analyses do is cut the margin of those errors; they cannot eliminate them. And, if a presidential campaign is absolutely, 100 percent certain of the outcome, that's when it is time to panic.

By mid-October, that time had arrived.

Hillary Clinton was still *below* the Plurality Threshold in Florida, Maine, Nevada, North Carolina, Minnesota, Ohio, New Hampshire and Wisconsin. She was *above* the threshold but by only half a percent in Michigan and Pennsylvania. Those 10 states were crucial blocks in the Blue Wall that Obama's victories in 2008 and 2012 had built.

The third-party candidates were holding their own—together they were drawing between 7 percent to 10 percent in those battleground states. And the undecided voters in those ten states ranged from a low of 2.8 percent in Ohio to high of 9.7 percent in Michigan.

How the undecided voters broke—toward Clinton or toward Trump—would ultimately decide the 2016 election. But what jobless households had endured, even those who had found good jobs that matched their skills, set the stage for how those undecideds voted in November. The unemployed, underemployed and uncounted had long memories and their angst and anxiety and frustration were driving the mood of the entire American electorate. They were "the why" behind those battleground states being so competitive.

Hillary Clinton could not undo what had been done. She could not erase those painful memories. She could not, even if she had tried, have rewritten the history of the last eight years, a history those jobless households shared and knew by heart, a history of betrayal by the party of Roosevelt and Truman, a history that would have infuriated John F. Kennedy and his brother Robert F. Kennedy, a history that saw the key constituencies of their Democratic Party abandoned throughout the Great Recession.

Others, particularly those who had ignored the "invisibles," had broken with the party's tradition of standing up for the little guy and gal. That betrayal was shattering the Democratic base into a million sharp-edged pieces. Now, as the Democratic nominee, Hillary owned the shards.

Those shards were about to draw blood. Hers.

CHAPTER 37

ON THE MARGINS

… 900 days ago, I got my "package" and realized that there was a good chance that I'd never get another decent job. A fire took care of my possessions a few months later and, today, I'm trying to limp to retirement age so that I can get Medicare. Depression? That's only a part of it. The last 25 years of my life were spent committed to an organization I believed in. They used me; I got paid. When I saw that white folder, though, I thought I was going to "stroke-out." Sweat poured across the back of my neck, I wondered if I'd give them the pleasure of watching me die right in front of them.

Thomas's Unemployment Story

So go ahead. Blame the white working class for Donald Trump's victory. Believe, if you will, that this demographic voted against its own interests once again. But also give them a little credit. In a way that our Democracy allows—no, encourages—they registered a massive protest vote.

Nationwide exit polls report that white non-college voters split 28 percent to 67 percent in favor of Donald Trump. As one-third (34 percent) of all voters, they cast 29 million votes for the bombastic and bigoted billionaire, nearly half (48.1 percent) of his votes. For Hillary Clinton that 39 percent margin was a killer; it was a wider defeat than George McGovern's in 1972 or Walter Mondale's in 1984.

Those statistics are deceptive. The Electoral College, not the popular vote, determines the winner. But much can be learned by analyzing the margins in each state. Trump's vote margins—as narrow as 10,700 votes in Michigan and as wide as 807,000 in Texas—show that he outperformed Mitt Romney in every red state save Arizona, Kansas, Texas and Utah.

In the big blue and battleground states, Trump easily exceeded Romney's margins and won Florida, Pennsylvania, Ohio, Michigan, North Carolina and Wisconsin. Trump's combined margin in those six states was 817,000 votes of which 446,000 votes, or 55 percent, came from a single state: Ohio. One can easily argue that had Sherrod Brown been the Democratic vice presidential nominee that wipeout would never have occurred.

And were it not for California, Hillary Clinton's nationwide margin in the popular vote would have been a negative number. The Golden State outperformed even its powerful showings in the last three election cycles by 1.6 million votes! Its 4.3 million vote margin was nearly twice that of New York and New Jersey combined.

What happened in the 19 states of the "red team strategy"? Trump's campaign slashed the Obama–Biden margins by more than 25 percent— the core assumption in my memos—in 15 states. Only in California, Massachusetts, Washington and the District of Columbia did he underperform the "red team strategy" projections.

Nor did that massive compression of Obama–Biden margins sneak up on the Clinton campaign. I had e-mailed John Podesta on June 8, August

30 and September 28 describing how Hillary's margins kept shrinking. The final e-mail on the "red team strategy" underscored the growing threat:

> "The latest *RealClear Politics* polling averages indicate that my 'red team strategy' is working ... all to[o] fucking well for Trump.
>
> **The margins in the 18 bluest states plus DC have shrunk so dramatically that Obama's 4 million vote victory in the popular vote four years ago has been erased. Those RCP polling averages now put Hillary 645,000 votes BELOW the president's performance back in 2012 ...**
>
> **Four factors could alter these dismal blue state margins: a large uneven split in the undecided vote; the withering of support for the third party candidates; a couple more debate fiascos by Trump; and a concerted effort to drive up Democratic turnout in those 19 states."**

I shared that final e-mail and Podesta's "Thx, Rick" reply with three dozen key labor leaders and progressive activists in the forlorn hope that it might shock them out of their complacency. Only Mike Lux, then working for Donna Brazile at the Democratic National Committee, acted on this WARN notice. Lux convinced her to start moving money into a few of those blue states.

It was too late.

The RCP polling averages as of the September 28 e-mail had the margins down to 0.5 percent in Florida (a 71 percent haircut from 2012), down to 1.8 percent in Pennsylvania (an 81 percent haircut), down to 4.7 percent in Michigan (a 79 percent haircut), down to 0.9 percent in North Carolina (a 79 percent haircut) and down to 4.3 percent in Minnesota (again a 71 percent haircut). Wisconsin, which did not have a top-25 media market and therefore was not included in the "red team strategy," saw its

6.9 percent margin in 2012 go negative (−0.7 percent) in September 2016. At those levels, it was less of a haircut and more of a decapitation.

Trump won Pennsylvania by 44,300 votes, Michigan by 10,700 and Wisconsin by 22,700—a combined margin of 78,000 votes. Flipping those three states gave him an Electoral College victory. In those three states, the infamous U-6, the broadest measure of unemployment, was *still* over 10 percent. And *official* unemployment had actually *increased* in 2016 from 279,000 to 318,000 in Pennsylvania. In Michigan it also *increased* in 2016 from 201,000 to 218,000. In Wisconsin, it *decreased* during 2016 from 129,000 to 112,000. But then *official* unemployment was always half that of *real* unemployment.

On election day, the *official* unemployment in Florida was 497,000, U-6 was 10.3 percent and Clinton lost the Sunshine State by 112,000 votes. In Ohio, the *official* unemployment was 250,000, U-6 was 9.6 percent and Clinton lost the Buckeye State by 446,000 votes. In North Carolina, the *official* unemployment was 234,000, U-6 was 9.8 percent and Clinton lost the Tarheel State by 173,000 votes. Only in Minnesota, where the *official* unemployment had *increased* to 96,000 in 2016 and U-6 stood at 8 percent was Clinton able to win the Gopher State by 44,000 votes—180,000 fewer than Obama in 2012 and 253,000 fewer than him in 2008.

In the six battleground states that Clinton lost, the unemployed, underemployed and uncounted had had it. Even though things *were* getting better, the memories of what they and their families went through were fresh and vivid. Just 30 months earlier, voters in those states still felt the pain of the broadest measure of unemployment. U-6 was still 14.3 percent in Florida, 15.2 percent in Michigan, 13.6 percent in North Carolina, 13.1 percent in Ohio, 13 percent in Pennsylvania and 11.7 percent in Wisconsin.

Hillary Clinton was either the Secretary of State or a private citizen during the worst years of the Great Recession. She had zero responsibility for those unemployment numbers—*official*, U-6 or *real* unemployment—but the Democratic Party did. Democratic governors, members of Congress and senators did. Vice President Joe Biden did. President Barack Obama did. And their acts of omission triggered fresh and vivid memories in jobless households with every Trump tweet and rally.

For, even as Hillary Clinton was winning the popular vote by 2.9 million votes, Trump was siphoning off white working class Democratic votes, depressing turnout among the "rising America electorate," and riling up the red states in a way Romney was never capable of doing. In the end, it was the defections by working class Democrats that doomed Hillary's candidacy.

Hillary Clinton was never going to win the white working class. No Democratic nominee has done so since Bill Clinton in 1992. But neither did she have to lose those non-college men and women by a margin of 39 points. That is all on her and her campaign.

Hillary for America was a misnomer. The campaign consciously ignored one-third of the electorate . . . in both the general election and the primaries. It was a deliberate decision, a decision taken against the advice of a master strategist—Bill Clinton. The former president, who had faced the voters twenty-one times and lost only twice, was laughed at, reportedly, by aides who had never run for office.

They're not laughing now.

Not only did Hillary Clinton lose the white working class vote by 37 points, she lost it by 11 more points than Barrack Obama did in 2012 and 19 points more than he did in 2008. Racial intolerance did not drive those numbers. Indifference did. Neglect did.

Neither a political party nor its presidential candidates can turn their backs on the plight of a core constituency, repeatedly, and expect to be rewarded with their votes. For millions of white working class Democrats, the 2016 campaign was the last straw. They sent an unmistakable and obscene message: screw you.

That they did.

America's unemployed, however, had been a swing vote since 2008. Their slide from comfortably middle class to working class or even into the non-working class was swift and their recovery, if any, was snail-like—slow, uncertain and slippery. In the midterm elections of 2010 and 2014, they narrowly supported Democratic congressional candidates. In the presidential elections of 2008 and 2012, those jobless households gave Barack Obama double-digit margins fully expecting him to deliver on his promises of jobs and economic growth and more than willing to punish Republicans for their opposition to the stimulus and for holding them hostage to their all-so-precious tax cuts.

For seven interminable years, unemployed Americans went from hope to hopelessness, from disbelief to despair. They had sent out hundreds, if not thousands of resumes, with barely an acknowledgment e-mail. They had called and written their elected officials and, if they were fortunate, received computer-generated replies. They had lost almost a decade of their earning potential even as their assets dwindled away to nothing. They watched the Wall Street Wizards get their bonuses despite wrecking the economy, and the stock market soar to new heights, making the rich all the more richer. Even though many had persevered with help from family and friends, they grew pessimistic about their prospects, disillusioned by the political process and more and more isolated from their *small d* Democratic traditions and their prior votes for Barack Obama.

In 2016, America's jobless households turned if ever so slightly toward the strong man, the man on the white horse, the man who promised to "Make America Great Again." Once again, they found themselves the swing vote—they kept swinging back and forth between the two major candidates. They no longer believed in hope and change. Neither did they believe in a monarchy of one. So they voted for change if they voted at all.

Deep down, however, they felt it was payback time. Revenge, they had been told time and time again, was a dish best served cold. By the time they hit the polling places on election day, they had waited long enough.

CHAPTER 38

A BRUTAL REMINDER

We are pretty worn out down here right now, so could you please bring back our jobs? A lot of us are old and have worked really hard for most of our lives, and we are finding it hard to find a new place where we can be productive and take care of our own lives.

Eleanor's Unemployment Story

Thirty-one million Americans shared the experience of being laid off, working part-time because they had to or remaining uncounted owing to statistical decisions by their government. That number was never static. Men and women moved between the various categories as the Great Recession unfolded. Some found work, often at much lower pay rates or salaries. Others prematurely retired or left the workforce entirely.

Over the last decade, those 31 million Americans were seared by the loss of self-identity that comes with not having a job. Some were out of work for months, others for years and years. To varying degrees, they cut back on expenses, tapped their savings, borrowed from friends and family. Some eventually lost their homes, their marriages, their self-confidence. For the first time in history, the death rate of white Americans, particularly those in working class communities, soared. Alcohol, drugs, depression and suicide were the grim reapers let loose by the Great Recession.

When they turned to their government for help, fewer than half of them qualified for unemployment insurance (UI). Others did qualify and, depending on which state they lived in and its rate of unemployment, they received $230 to $350 per week. The 99ers spent months trying to extend those UI benefits to a Tier 5 only to see a GOP-controlled Congress use unemployment as a bargaining chip for their wealthy contributors' tax cuts.

As the years wore on and the promised recovery sputtered along slowly but never really took off nor touched them, those 31 million Americans became more discouraged, more depressed and more cynical. The brief unemployed stories found at the beginning of each chapter were replicated in houses and apartments all across the land. The growing levels of tension, frustration and anger in those jobless households altered family dynamics—the older generation offered what help they could, the younger generation feared the outbursts but no one was left untouched by the experience.

Much like the assassinations of President John F. Kennedy, Reverend Martin Luther King, Jr., and Senator Robert F. Kennedy, everyone in those jobless households knew where they were the day when one of the family's breadwinners was laid off, downsized or right-sized. But the impact of that shared experience was dulled because the emotional pain—that sense of failure or that it was somehow "my fault"—was internalized and seldom verbalized to the outside world.

That sense of isolation that the Union of Unemployed tried to break grew with every minute spent surfing the Internet looking for work. It grew with every resume sent out and every screamingly silent rejection. It grew with every passing day until it became overpowering, until it colored every decision these men and women faced, until it became their entire lives and they withdrew from the personal connections they had enjoyed in better times.

The unemployed, underemployed and uncounted, eventually but never all at once, became the "necessitous men" that Franklin Delano Roosevelt spoke about in 1944. His State of the Union speech reminded Americans in his day (and ours) that,

> "We cannot be content, no matter how high that general standard of living may be, if some fraction of our people—whether it be one-third or one-fifth or one-tenth—is ill-fed, ill-clothed, ill-housed, and insecure.
>
> This Republic had its beginning, and grew to its present strength, under the protection of certain inalienable political rights—among them the right of free speech, free press, free worship, trial by jury, freedom from unreasonable searches and seizures. They were our rights to life and liberty.
>
> As our nation has grown in size and stature, however—as our industrial economy expanded—these political rights proved inadequate to assure us equality in the pursuit of happiness.
>
> We have come to a clear realization of the fact that true individual freedom cannot exist without economic security and independence. 'Necessitous men are not free men'. People who are hungry and out of a job are the stuff of which dictatorships are made.
>
> In our day these economic truths have become accepted as self-evident. We have accepted, so to speak, a second Bill of Rights under which a new basis of security and prosperity can be established for all—regardless of station, race, or creed.
>
> Among these are the following rights:
>
> The right to a useful and remunerative job in the industries or shops or farms or mines of the nation;

The right to earn enough to provide adequate food and clothing and recreation;

The right of every farmer to raise and sell his products at a return which will give him and his family a decent living;

The right of every businessman, large and small, to trade in an atmosphere of freedom from unfair competition and domination by monopolies at home or abroad;

The right of every family to a decent home;

The right to adequate medical care and the opportunity to achieve and enjoy good health;

The right to adequate protection from the economic fears of old age, sickness, accident, and unemployment;

The right to a good education.

All of these rights spell security. And after this war is won we must be prepared to move forward, in the implementation of these rights, to new goals of human happiness and well-being.

America's own rightful place in the world depends in large part upon how fully these and similar rights have been carried into practice for all our citizens. For unless there is security here at home there cannot be lasting peace in the world."

FDR knew that his Second Bill of Rights would not be adopted in his lifetime. Nor have any of his amendments to the US Constitution been officially proposed and placed before state legislatures for ratification or state ratifying conventions in the seven decades since his speech.

Those were FDR's ideals and ideas that had welded the generations of Americans who experienced the Great Depression to the Democratic Party. One shudders to think of the dressing down any political strategist would have received from Roosevelt for suggesting that his base be ignored in favor of a "rising American electorate." These were the same New Deal principles that jobless households of the last decade needed to have reaffirmed. Precisely nuanced words did not matter to them, but the willingness of a president or even their party's presidential nominee to stand with them could have generated the smallest glimmer of hope.

The presidential elections of 2008, 2012 and 2016 played out against a background of widespread economic turmoil. So, too, did the midterm elections of 2010 and 2014. And voters from jobless households made up at least one-third to two-fifths of the turnout depending on the year and the state. Unemployment might not have been the issue that campaign consultants focused on but it was the issue that drove millions of Americans to the polls.

When their hopes were dashed, those now necessitous men and women sought revenge. It was an all-too natural reaction when your family has been harmed. It was not something you shared with pollsters or exit poll interviewers. It was, however, something that you brooded about and contemplated in isolation. Or, as Charles Dickens put it in *A Tale of Two Cities*, "Vengeance and retribution require a long time; it is the rule."

Dickens' rule complimented another immutable rule of politics. Loyalty is a two-way street. When both those rules are ignored, disaster strikes, as it did in 2010, 2014 and again in 2016.

Democratic candidates, instead of following FDR's lead, had turned their backs on those voters who, after the waves of WARN notices started arriving in 2007 and Lehman Brothers collapsed in 2008, produced the surge that made Barack Obama president, increased Democratic majorities in the House and Senate and drove up the number of Democratic governors, state senators and state reps. Those surge voters were middle class and working class Democrats—whites, blacks, Latinos, Asians and Millennials. And each demographic found themselves hammered by the Great Recession.

They hailed his American Recovery and Reinvestment Act but were dismayed by the lack of a second stimulus. When all the focus shifted to the Affordable Care Act, many, far too many, began having second thoughts about the party of Franklin Delano Roosevelt. It required a heavy lift— and a huge miscue by Mitt Romney—to shift jobless households back to President Obama in 2012.

By 2016, the unemployed, underemployed and uncounted became the new "invisibles." They were not part of the "rising America electorate" that so captivated the strategists of Hillary Clinton's campaign. Nor were they worth considering for admission in the "coalition of the ascendant" for they were obviously on a downward trajectory. Even the exit polls ignored them; work status including being unemployed vanished from the questionnaire in 2016.

Donald Trump, however, scratched at the scab tissue that nearly a decade of joblessness had left on those 31 million Americans. With every tweet and rally, he picked at that wound until it bled. His opponents, Democratic and Republican alike, forgot FDR's warning that "people who are hungry and out of a job are the stuff of which dictatorships are made." They also forgot that hunger and joblessness is what motivates men and women to take revenge on their tormentors.

So now, the dish best served cold is empty. The revenge of America's unemployed helped elect a raging narcissist, an economic royalist of the first order and an incipient monarchy of one to the presidency. Only time will tell if his incomprehensible and indefensible policies will trigger a second recession, an even graver recession that buries the last vestiges of our democracy.

According to George Orwell, the author of *1984* and somewhat of an expert on authoritarian regimes, the revenge impulse recedes quickly. "The whole idea of revenge and punishment is a childish day-dream. Properly speaking, there is no such thing as revenge. Revenge is an act which you want to commit when you are powerless and because you are powerless: as soon as the sense of impotence is removed, the desire evaporates also."

Let us hold on to that thought even as we resist the Trump tantrums at every turn. Let us rely on the nemesis of authoritarian regimes, Franklin Delano Roosevelt, to guide us in a different direction. His State of the Union speech offers us reassurance and a compelling strategy going forward.

For it is within our power to turn those necessitous men and women into *small d* Democrats again, address their sense of economic insecurity and guarantee them that "prosperity can be established for all—regardless of station, race, or creed."

Then and only then, will they look to us for a champion.

NOTES

Preface Be Their Champion

Van Horn, C., Zukin,C. and Sewell, R. (2014). Left Behind: The Long-term Unemployed Struggle in an Improving Economy. Rutgers University's John J. Heldrich Center for Workforce Development. Retrieved from http://www.heldrich. rutgers.edu/products/left-behind-long-term-unemployed-struggle-improving-economy.

Chapter 1 - Crying Wolf

United States. Federal Reserve Board. (2007 to 2011). Full Timeline of the Financial Crisis. Retrieved from the Federal Reserve Bank of St. Louis website: https://www.stlouisfed.org/financial-crisis/full-timeline.

United States. Department of Labor (2009, March). Extended Mass Layoffs in 2007. Retrieved from the Department of Labor website: https://www.bls.gov/opub/reports/mass-layoffs/archive/extended_mass_layoffs2007.pdf

United States. Department of Labor. (2013, June 21). Mass layoff events and initial claimants for unemployment insurance, June 2009 to May 2013, seasonally adjusted. Retrieved from the Department of Labor website: https://www.bls.gov/news.release/mmls.t01.htm.

United States. Department of Labor. (Undated). The Worker Adjustment and Retraining Notification Act: A Guide to Advance

Notice of Closings and Layoffs. Retrieved from the Department of Labor website: https://www.dol.gov/general/topic/termination/plantclosings.

Chapter 2 - Conversations with the Candidates

Sloan, R. (2007). Choices '08: Conversations with the Candidates. IAM Journal. Volume 13, Number 3.

Taft-Hartley Section 14(b). (n.d) In Wikipedia, retrieved December 12, 2015 from https://en.wikipedia.org/wiki/Right-to-work_law.

United States. National Labor Relations Board. (Undated). Retrieved from the NLRB website: https://www.nlrb.gov/who-we-are/our-history/1947-taft-hartley-substantive-provisions.

Hogler, R. (2015, September 7). Happy anniversary, right-to-work, but it's time to go. The Hill. Retrieved from http://thehill.com/blogs/pundits-blog/labor/252620-happy-anniversary-right-to-work-but-its-time-to-go.

Chapter 3 - America's Strength

Unnamed Author. (2008). America's Edge: Skills. IAM Journal. Volume 14, Number 1.

Unnamed Author. (2007, November 20). IAM to Launch America's Edge Campaign. IMAIL. Retrieved from https://www.goiam.org/news/imail-for-tuesday-november-20-2007/.

Unnamed Author. (2008, January 31). America's Edge Campaign Reaps Big Dividends. IMAIL. Retrieved from https://www.goiam.org/news/imail-for-thursday-january-31-2008/.

Chapter 5 - Counting on Clinton

Unnamed Authors. (2008). Democratic Party presidential primaries, 1984 to 2008. wikipedia.org. Retrieved from https://en.wikipedia.org/wiki/Democratic_Party_presidential_primaries,_2008, https://en.wikipedia.org/wiki/Democratic_Party_presidential_primaries,_2004, https://en.wikipedia.org/wiki/Democratic_Party_presidential_primaries,_2000, https://en.wikipedia.org/wiki/Democratic_Party_presidential_primaries,_1992, https://en.wikipedia.org/wiki/Democratic_Party_presidential_primaries,_1988, https://en.wikipedia.org/wiki/Democratic_Party_presidential_primaries,_1984.

Chapter 6 - Riding Giant Waves

Dixon, C. (2008, January 9). Surfers Defy Giant Waves Awakened by Storm. New York Times. Retrieved from http://www.nytimes.com/2008/01/09/sports/othersports/09surf.html.

Unnamed Author. (2008, June). 2008 Democratic Delegates. Real Clear Politics. Retrieved from http://www.realclearpolitics.com/epolls/2008/president/democratic_delegate_count.html.

Chapter 7 - Convention for a Champion

Hillary Clinton, Text of Hillary Clinton Concession Speech. (speech, Washington, DC, June 7, 2008) The Guardian, https://www.theguardian.com/commentisfree/2008/jun/07/hillaryclinton.uselections20081.

Edward M. Kennedy, "2008 Democratic National Convention Speech" (speech, Denver, CO, August 25, 2008), American Rhetoric, http://www.americanrhetoric.com/speeches/convention2008/tedkennedy2008dnc.htm.

Edwards M. Kennedy, "1980 Democratic National Convention Speech" (speech, New York, NY August 12, 1980) American Rhetoric, http://www.americanrhetoric.com/speeches/tedkennedy1980dnc.htm.

Barack Obama, (2008, August 28). "Transcript of Barack Obama's Acceptance Speech" (speech, Denver, CO, August 28, 2008), New York Times, http://www.nytimes.com/2008/08/28/us/politics/28text-obama.html

Chapter 8 - More Gold Than Fort Knox

Mathaison, N. (2008, December 27). Three weeks that changed the world. The Guardian. Retrieved from https://www.theguardian.com/business/2008/dec/28/markets-credit-crunch-banking-2008.

Chapter 9 - Thirty Million

Isadore, C. (2008, December 19). Bush announces auto rescue. CNN Money. Retrieved from http://money.cnn.com/2008/12/19/news/companies/auto_crisis/.

Herszenhorn, D. and Sanger, D. (2008, December 11). Senate Abandons Automaker Bailout Bid. New York Times. Retrieved from http://www.nytimes.com/2008/12/12/business/12auto.html.

Chapter 10 - A Second Stimulus

Obama. B. (2009, January 20). President Barack Obama's Inaugural Address. The White House. Retrieved from https://www.whitehouse.gov/blog/2009/01/21/president-barack-obamas-inaugural-address.

Unnamed Author. (2009, January 21). Nearly 37.8 Million Watch President Obama's Oath and Speech. nelson.com. Retrieved from http://www.nielsen.com/us/en/insights/news/2009/nearly-378-million-watch-president-obamas-oath-and-speech.html.

Yourish, K and Stanton, L. (2009, February 1). Taking Apart the $819 billion Stimulus Package. Washington Post. Retrieved from http://www.washingtonpost.com/wp-dyn/content/graphic/2009/02/01/GR2009020100154.html.

Herszenhorn, D. (2009, February 13). Recovery Bill Gets Final Approval. New York Times. Retrieved from http://www.nytimes.com/2009/02/14/us/politics/14web-stim.html?_r=0&pagewanted=print.

Sahadi, J. (2009, February 15). Senate votes to approve the historic legislation aimed at reviving the economy. CNN Money. Retrieved from http://money.cnn.com/2009/02/13/news/economy/house_final_stimulus/index.htm?iid=EL.

Buffenbarger, R. (2009, February 8). U.S. jobs worth fighting for. Chicago Tribune. Retrieved from http://articles.chicagotribune.com/2009-02-08/news/0902070423_1_manufacturing-sector-global-recession-stimulus-package.

Biden, J. (2009, September 3). Vice President Joe Biden Addresses the Recovery Act at the Brookings Institution. Washington Post. Retrieved from http://www.washingtonpost.com/wp-dyn/content/article/2009/09/03/AR2009090301848.html.

United States. Congressional Budget Office. (2015, February 20). Estimated Impact of the American Recovery and Reinvestment Act on Employment and Economic Output in 2014. Retrieved from the CBO website: https://www.cbo.gov/publication/49958.

Chapter 11 - Jobs Now

Buffenbarger, R. (2009, May 15). Remarks at the National Labor College. GOIAM.org. Retrieved from (https://www.goiam.org/news/remarks-by-tom-buffenbarger-international-president-international-association-of-machinists-and-aerospace-workers-at-the-nation-al-labor-college-silver-spring-md.

Unnamed Author. (2009, Summer) Jobs Now. IAM Journal. Volume 14, Number 2. Retrieved from https://www.goiam.org/wp-content/uploads/2009/07/uploadedFiles_IAM_Journal_Summer_2009_Cover_JobsNOW.pdf.

Egwuekwe, L. (2009). Geography of a Recession. GOIAM.org. Retrieved from http://www.latoyaegwuekwe.com/geographyofarecession.html.

Unnamed Authors. (2009, July) Call for a National JOBS Now! Initiative - An Agenda to Put Americans Back to Work. AFL-CIO. Retrieved from http://www.aflcio.org/content/download/6848/74044/file/2009res_20amend.pdf.

Buffenbarger, R. (2009, November 6). Remarks at No Limits Conference. GOIAM.org. Retrieved from https://www.goiam.org/news/remarks-by-r-thomas-buffenbarger-at-the-no-limits-public-policy-conference/.

United States. Department of Labor. (2009, January 9). The Employment Situation: December 2008. Bureau of Labor Statistics. Retrieved from http://www.bls.gov/news.release/archives/empsit_01092009.pdf.

Chapter 12 - Building a Virtual Union

Bell, T. and Richardson, W. (2014, September 23). Great Northern Paper Files for Bankruptcy. Press Herald. Retrieved from http://www.pressherald.com/2014/09/23/great-northern-paper-files-for-bankruptcy/.

Kelber, H. (2010, February 23). The Unemployed Now Have Their Own Union, And It's Catching on Quickly. AlterNet. Retrieved from http://www.alternet.org/story/145797/the_unemployed_now_have_their_own_union,_and_it's_catching_on_quickly.

Sloan, R. (2010, June 15). Ensure Domestic Tranquility. Huffington Post. Retrieved from http://www.huffingtonpost.com/rick-sloan/ensure-domestic-tranquili_b_610506.html

Sifry, M. (2010, July 20). How the Internet Organizes the Unemployed. TechPresident. Retrieved from http://techpresident.com/blog-entry/how-internet-organizes-unemployed.

Piven, F. (2010, December 10-17). Mobilizing the Jobless. The Nation. Retrieved from https://www.thenation.com/article/mobilizing-jobless.

Chapter 13 - Time is Running Out

Sloan, R. (2010, May 12). In Politics, It's All About Timing, and Democratic Governors Could Use Some. Huffington Post. Retrieved from http://www.huffingtonpost.com/rick-sloan/in-politics-its-all-about_b_497294.html.

Chapter 15 - Keystone to Victory

Bureau of Labor Statistics, (2010 December 7). Unemployment in November 2010, Department of Labor. Retrieved from http://www.bls.gov/opub/ted/2010/ted_20101207.htm.

Totten, G. (2010, May 11). UCubed Campaign Ad for Pennsylvania. GOIAM. Retrieved from https://www.youtube.com/watch?v=BTuJXYOxZOc.

Sloan, R. (2010, June 1). Incumbents Better Take Note. Huffington Post. Retrieved from http://www.huffingtonpost.com/rick-sloan/incumbents-better-take-no_b_593938.html.

Chapter 17 - Last (Sad) Laughs

Thompson, K. and Gardner, A. (2010, November 3). Victories give force to tea party movement, The Washington Post, retrieved from http://www.washingtonpost.com.

Unnamed Graphic Artist, (2010 November 4). How the Tea Party Fared. New York Times. Retrieved from http://www.nytimes.com/interactive/2010/11/04/us/politics/tea-party-results.html?_r=0.

Unnamed Graphic Artist. (2010). Red Tide: Huge Changes in the Midterm Election, p2010.org. Retrieved from http://www.p2012.org/2010/.

Karpowitz, C. (2011, April. Tea Time in America? The Impact of the Tea Party Movement on the 2010 Midterm Elections. PS: Political Science & Politics, Vol. 44, Issue 02. Retrieved from http://journalistsresource.org/studies/politics/elections/tea-party-movement-2010-midterm-elections.

Chapter 18 - Humor Works

Krugman, P. (2011, May 30). Against Learned Helplessness. New York Times. Retrieved from http://www.nytimes.com/2011/05/30/opinion/30krugman.html.

Unnamed Author. (2010, November 29). Stabenow Calls for Passage of Tier V Unemployment Extension Bill, Lemieux Objects. The Huffington Post. Retrieved from http://www.huffingtonpost.com/wires/2010/09/29/stabenow-calls-for-passag_ws_744269.html.

Stone, C. (2010, December 6). New Findings Show Unemployment Insurance Trumps High-Income Tax Cuts on Jobs, Deficits. Center on Budget Policies & Priorities. Retrieved from http://www.cbpp.org/

blog/new-findings-show-unemployment-insurance-trumps-high-income-tax-cuts-on-jobs-deficits.

Halloran, L. (2013, December 7). Obama's Tax Cut Deal: So Much For Deficit Reduction. NPR. Retrieved from: http://www.npr.org/2010/12/07/131879993/obama-s-tax-cut-deal-so-much-for-deficit-reduction.

Montgomery, L., Murray, S. and Branigin, W. (2010, December 17). Obama signs bill to extend Bush-era tax cuts for two more years. Washington Post. Retrieved from http://www.washingtonpost.com/wp-dyn/content/article/2010/12/16/AR2010121606200_3.html?sid=ST2011022703543

Chapter 19 - Where's MY Job, Mr. President

Teixeira, R. (2011 June 19). The White Working Class: The Group That Will Likely Decide Obama's Fate. The New Republic. Retrieved from https://newrepublic.com/article/90241/obama-election-2012.

Taylor, N. (2009). The Enduring Legacy of the WPA: When FDR Put the Nation to Work. New York: Penguin RandomHouse.

Chapter 20 - Coalition of the Ascendant

Teixeira, R. and Halpin, J. (2011 November). The Path to 270: Demographics versus Economics in the 2012 Presidential Election. Center for American Progress. Retrieved from https://www.americanprogress.org/wp-content/uploads/issues/2011/11/pdf/path_to_270.pdf.

Edsall, T. (2011 November 27). The Future of the Obama Coalition. New York Times. Retrieved from https://campaignstops.blogs.nytimes.com/2011/11/27/the-future-of-the-obama-coalition/.

United States. Department of Labor. (2011, October 7). The Employment Situation — September 2011. Retrieved from the Bureau of Labor Statistics website: http://www.bls.gov/news.release/archives/empsit_10072011.pdf.

Chapter 22 - Breakout Year

Stolberg, G. and McIntire, M. (2013, October 5). A Federal Budget Crisis Months in the Planning. New York Times. Retrieved from http://www.nytimes.com/2013/10/06/us/a-federal-budget-crisis-months-in-the-planning.html.

Chapter 24 - The Invisibles

Hillary Clinton, "Excerpt from Hillary Clinton's Remarks at the New Hampshire Democratic Party's "100 Club" Dinner," (speech, Manchester, NH, March 10, 2007) Online by Gerhard Peters and John T. Woolley, The American Presidency Project, http://www.presidency.ucsb.edu/ws/?pid=96356.

Chapter 26 - Assault on the Chameleons

United States. Department of Labor. (2017, February 23). Not in the Labor Force. Labor Force Statistics from the Current Population Survey. Retrieved from the Bureau of Labor Statistics: https://data.bls.gov/timeseries/LNS15000000.

Chapter 27 - Hit With A Two By Four

Hindery, L. (2014, September 8). Glum and Glummer: Democrats and Voters) Keep Overlooking Jobless Households. Huffington Post. Retrieved from http://www.huffingtonpost.com/leo-hindery-jr/glum-and-glummer-democrat_b_5784130.html.

Chapter 28 - GOP Infrastructure Growth

File, T. (2015, July). Who Votes? Congressional Elections and the American Electorate: 1978–2014. U. S. Census. Retrieved from http://www.census.gov/content/dam/Census/library/publications/2015/demo/p20-577.pdf.

Unnamed Author. (2016). Barack Obama: Vetoed legislation. Ballotpedia. Retrieved from the Ballotpedia website: https://ballotpedia.org/Barack_Obama:_Vetoed_legislation.

Chapter 30 - Working Class Democrats

Chozick, A. (2015, April 12). Hillary Clinton Announces 2016 Presidential Bid. New York Times. Retrieved from https://www.nytimes.com/2015/04/13/us/politics/hillary-clinton-2016-presidential-campaign.html?_r=0.

Chozick, A. (2015, April 12). Hillary Clintons Announcement Video. New York Times. Retrieved from https://www.nytimes.com/video/us/politics/100000003624500/hillary-clintons-announcement-video.html.

Frizell, S. (2015, June 13). Transcript: Read the Full Text of Hillary Clinton's Campaign Launch Speech. Time. Retrieved from http://time.com/3920332/transcript-full-text-hillary-clinton-campaign-launch/.

Mellman, M. (2015, August 11). Findings From A Survey Of 600 Working-Class Democrats In The Pre-Primary States. Union of Unemployed. Retrieved from www.ucubed2016.org.